PECOS BILL

The Perpetual Motion Ranch

PECOS BILL
The Greatest Cowboy of All Time

By

JAMES CLOYD BOWMAN

Author of

Tales from a Finnish Tupa
The Adventures of Paul Bunyan, etc.

Pictures by
LAURA BANNON

ALBERT WHITMAN & CO.
CHICAGO   ILLINOIS

TO

THE AMERICAN COWBOY

CONCERNING

THE TALL TALES

OF

PECOS BILL

This is a volume of genuine American folklore. For years the author has made folklore his hobby. He has collected these stories from many and varied sources. He has had access to the largest collections of original documents left by the early adventurers into the open Range Country. He has gleaned facts from the fabulous story tellers, whose hearts have swelled with the expansive joys of the unexplored West. He has listened to the yarns of present-day cowboys, whose imagination has been stirred by broad frontier humor.

The author wishes to express his thanks to the following persons who have interested themselves in his research: the officers of the Harvard University Library, who gave him permission to work in the stacks among their original documents; Philip Ashton Rollins, author of *THE COWBOY: HIS EQUIPMENT, AND HIS PART IN THE DEVELOPMENT OF THE WEST;* Dr. J. Frank Dobie, Secretary of the Texas Folklore Society; Tex O'Reilly, creator of Pecos Bill yarns; Harry Benge Crozier, Editor of *THE CATTLEMAN;* J. Marvin Hunter, Editor of the *FRONTIER TIMES;* E. W. Winkler, Librarian of the University of Texas; and Charles E. Brown of Madison, Wisconsin, authority on western folklore.

These adventures of Pecos Bill constitute a part of the Saga of the Cowboy. They are collected from the annals of the campfire and the roundup. They preserve the glory of the days when men were men, and when imagination and wonder rode hand in hand to conquest and to undying fame.

These tales are vital examples of the broad humor of America that has been long in the making. The bigness of the virgin frontier expanded the imagination of the first settlers, and the hardness of the life developed their self-reliance.

Before 1800, these forefathers were singing *Yankee Doodle,* and jigging and laughing and laying bets to see who could add the most nonsensical stanza to the humorous ballad.

As civilization swept over the Appalachians, and decades later, as it again swept across the Mississippi, the expansive individualism of the frontiersmen grew by leaps and bounds. Truth soon became entirely too small for the new, strange environment, and men began to exaggerate with the zest and amusement of small boys in seeing how nimble they could keep their wits and how flexible their imagination.

The frontiersmen thus freed themselves from the drab, cruel world of hardship and tragedy which encompassed them every-where. One tall tale naturally led to a taller tale, until every strange situation and every untoward experience of the backwoods was given a fresh glamor, as wonderful as the beauty and the strangeness of the ancient world of Greek mythology or the Age of Chivalry. It was in this manner that the frontiersmen saved their souls and prevented their bodies and minds from succumbing to the entire want of luxury and the stint of comfort.

To rightly give this imaginative world of their creation a definite form and substance, they added the charm of fictitious narrative and mythical characters. During each decade they reorganized their wild yarns about some popular hero such as Daniel Boone or Davy Crockett. And the hearty laughter that ensued from their wild exploits of fancy did them good like a medicine.

During the last three decades of the nineteenth century our civilization opened two new frontiers and added two new heroes of Gargantuan proportions. When the great armies of lumberjacks swung singing into the virgin forests, they found an outlet for their suddenly released imagination in Paul Bunyan; and when, about the same time, other great armies of singing cowboys galloped into the Range Country of the Southwest, they created Pecos Bill. Paul Bunyan and Pecos Bill are not only between themselves blood-brothers, but they are also brothers to Daniel Boone and Davy Crockett, as well as to such lesser known figures as Blowing Cave, Nimrod Wildfire, and Sam Slick.

About the person of Pecos Bill have been told—and still are being told—the best of the tall yarns that have survived the old Frontier days. Pecos Bill is a gentleman at heart, and directs his course by the common-sense, homely virtues of the Frontier. He represents the best and most characteristic broad humor of America.

JAMES CLOYD BOWMAN.

TABLE OF CONTENTS

PART I

PECOS BILL BECOMES A COWBOY

PART II

MODERN COWPUNCHING IS INVENTED AND DEVELOPED

PART III

PECOS BILL ROAMS THE SOUTHWEST

TABLE OF CONTENTS—*Continued*

PART IV

The Passing of Pecos Bill

FULL PAGE ILLUSTRATIONS

COLOR PLATES

BLACK AND WHITE PLATES

PECOS BILL

Pecos Bill

PART I

PECOS BILL BECOMES A COWBOY

Migrating to the Rio Grande

I.

PECOS BILL BECOMES A COYOTE

PECOS BILL had the strangest and most exciting experience any boy ever had. He became a member of a pack of wild Coyotes, and until he was a grown man, believed that his name was Cropear, and that he was a full-blooded Coyote. Later he discovered that he was a human being and very shortly thereafter became the greatest cowboy of all time. This is how it all came about.

Pecos Bill's family was migrating westward through Texas

29

in the early days, in an old covered wagon with wheels made from cross sections of a sycamore log. His father and mother were riding in the front seat, and his father was driving a wall-eyed, spavined roan horse and a red and white spotted milch cow hitched side by side. The eighteen children in the back of the wagon were making such a medley of noises that their mother said it wasn't possible even to hear thunder.

Just as the wagon was rattling down to the ford across the Pecos River, the rear left wheel bounced over a great piece of rock, and Bill, his red hair bristling like porcupine quills, rolled out of the rear of the wagon, and landed, up to his neck, in a pile of loose sand. He was only four years old at the time, and he lay dazed until the wagon had crossed the river and had disappeared into the sage brush. It wasn't until his mother rounded up the family for the noonday meal that Bill was missed. The last anyone remembered seeing him was just before they had forded the river.

The mother and eight or ten of the older children hurried back to the river and hunted everywhere, but they could find no trace of the lost boy. When evening came, they were forced to go back to the covered wagon, and later, to continue their journey without him. Ever after, when they thought of Bill, they remembered the river, and so they naturally came to speak of him as Pecos Bill.

What had happened to Bill was this. He had strayed off into the mesquite, and a few hours later was found by a wise old Coyote, who was the undisputed leader of the Loyal and Approved Packs of the Pecos and Rio Grande Valleys. He was, in fact, the Granddaddy of the entire race of Coyotes, and so his followers, out of affection to him, called him Grandy.

When he accidentally met Bill, Grandy was curious, but shy.

He sniffed and he yelped, and he ran this way and that, the better to get the scent, and to make sure there was no danger. After a while he came quite near, sat up on his haunches, and waited to see what the boy would do. Bill trotted up to Grandy and began running his hands through the long, shaggy hair.

"What a nice old doggie you are," he repeated again and again.

"Yes, and what a nice Cropear you are," yelped Grandy joyously.

And so, ever after, the Coyotes called the child Cropear.

Grandy was much pleased with his find and so, by running ahead and stopping and barking softly, he led the boy to the jagged side of Cabezon, or the Big Head, as it was called. This was a towering mass of mountain that rose abruptly, as if by magic, from the prairie. Around the base of this mountain the various families of the Loyal and Approved Packs had burrowed out their dens.

Here, far away from the nearest human dwelling, Grandy made a home for Cropear, and taught him all the knowledge of the wild out-of-doors. He led Cropear to the berries that were good to eat, and dug up roots that were sweet and spicy. He showed the boy how to break open the small nuts from the piñon; and when Cropear wanted a drink, he led him to a vigorous young mother Coyote who gave him of her milk. Cropear thus drank in the very life blood of a thousand generations of wild life and became a native beast of the prairie, without at all knowing that he was a man-child.

Grandy became his teacher and schooled him in the knowledge that had been handed down through thousands of generations of the Pack's life. He taught Cropear the many signal calls, and the code of right and wrong, and the gentle art of loyalty to the leader. He also trained him to leap long distances and to dance; and to flip-flop and to twirl his body so fast that the eye could not follow his movements. And most important of all, he instructed him in the silent, rigid pose of invisibility, so that he could see all that was going on around him without being seen.

And as Cropear grew tall and strong, he became the pet of the Pack. The Coyotes were always bringing him what they thought he would like to eat, and were ever showing him the many secrets of the fine art of hunting. They taught him where the Field-mouse nested, where the Song Thrush hid her eggs, where the Squirrel stored his nuts; and where the Mountain Sheep concealed their young among the towering rocks.

When the Jack-rabbit was to be hunted, they gave Cropear his station and taught him to do his turn in the relay race. And when the prong-horn Antelope was to be captured, Cropear took his place among the encircling pack and helped bring the fleeting animal to bay and pull him down, in spite of his darting, charging antlers.

Grandy took pains to introduce Cropear to each of the animals and made every one of them promise he would not harm the growing man-child. "Au-g-gh!" growled the Mountain Lion, "I will be as careful as I can. But be sure to tell your child to be careful, too!"

"Gr-r-rr!" growled the fierce Grizzly Bear, "I have crunched many a marrow bone, but I will not harm your boy. Gr-r-rr!"

"Yes, we'll keep our perfumery and our quills in our inside vest pockets," mumbled the silly Skunk and Porcupine, as if suffering from adenoids.

But when Grandy talked things over with the Bull Rattle-

The Wouser

snake, he was met with the defiance of hissing rattles. "Nobody will ever make me promise to protect anybody or anything! S-s-s-s-ss! I'll do just as I please!"

"Be careful of your wicked tongue," warned Grandy, "or you'll be very sorry."

But when Grandy met the Wouser, things were even worse. The Wouser was a cross between the Mountain Lion and the Grizzly Bear, and was ten times larger than either. Besides that, he was the nastiest creature in the world. "I can only give you fair warning," yowled the Wouser, "and if you prize your man-child, as you say you do, you will have to keep him out of harm's way!" And as the Wouser continued, he stalked back and forth, lashing his tail and gnashing his jaws, and acting as if he were ready to snap somebody's head off. "What's more, you know that nobody treats me as a friend. Everybody runs around behind my back spreading lies about me. Everybody says I carry hydrophobia—the deadly poison—about on my person, and because of all these lies, I am shunned like a leper. Now you come sneaking around asking me to help you. Get out of my sight before I do something I shall be sorry for!"

"I'm not sneaking," barked Grandy in defiance, "and besides, you're the one who will be sorry in the end."

So it happened that all the animals, save only the Bull Rattlesnake and the Wouser, promised to help Cropear bear a charmed life so that no harm should come near him. And by good fortune, the boy was never sick. The vigorous exercise and the fresh air and the constant sunlight helped him to become the healthiest, strongest, most active boy in the world.

All this time Cropear was growing up in the belief that he

was a full-blooded Coyote. Long before he had grown to manhood, he learned to understand the language of every creeping, hopping, walking, and flying creature; and, boylike, he began to amuse himself by mimicking every animal of his acquaintance. He soon learned to trill and warble like a Mocking Bird, and to growl like a Grizzly Bear. He could even yowl like a Wouser and sputter like a stupid Skunk.

The Coyotes didn't much like this mimic language, for they were never sure whether they were hearing a Sage Hen or a Buffalo or a Cricket, or whether it was merely Cropear at his play. But Cropear was so full of animal spirits and healthy mischief that he could never keep long from this sport. In time he became so expert as a mimic that he could confuse even the Rattlesnake or the Field-mouse or the Antelope. He could thus call any animal to himself, assume the rigid pose of invisibility, and completely deceive the cleverest creature alive.

By the time Cropear had become a man, he could run with the fleetest of the Coyotes. At night, he squatted on his haunches in the circle and barked and yipped and howled sadly, according to the best tradition of the Pack.

The Loyal and Approved Packs were proud, indeed, that they had made a man-child into a Noble Coyote, the equal of the best both in the hunt and in the inner circle where the laws and customs of the Pack were unfolded. They were prouder still that they had taught him to believe that the Human Race, to a greater extent than any other race of animals, was *inhuman*. Just what the Human Race was, Cropear never knew, however. For Grandy kept him far away even from the cowboys' trails.

As the years passed, the fame of Cropear spread widely, for

the proud Coyotes could not help bragging about him to everybody they met, and the other animals began to envy the clever Pack that had made the man-child into a Coyote. Naturally enough, Cropear became the chief surgeon of the Pack. When a cactus thorn or a porcupine quill lodged in the foot or imbedded itself in the muzzle of any of his brethren, Cropear, with his supple human hand, pulled it out.

Thus the years ran through their ceaseless glass, and the shadow of time lengthened among the Pack. Grandy, for all his wisdom, grew too feeble to follow the trail, too heavy and slow to pull down the alert, bounding prong-horn, or to nip the heels of the fleeting Buffalo Calf. His teeth loosened so that he could no longer tear the savory meat from the bone, or crunch out the juicy marrow.

Then one day Grandy went out alone to hunt and did not return; and everyone knew that he had gone down the long, long trail that has no turning.

But there was no longer need for anyone to help Cropear. He was sturdy and supple, swift as a bird in flight. Often he got the better of the Pack in the hunt and outwitted his brother Coyotes every day. Many of them began to wonder if they had done such a wise thing after all in making Cropear a member of their Pack.

II.

PECOS BILL DISCOVERS HE IS A HUMAN

Not long after Grandy's disappearance, a remarkable adventure befell Cropear. He was, at the time, hunting across the rolling mesa. He had just stopped to examine a stretch of grassy plain where the prairie dogs had built themselves a city. The prairie dogs were making merry as if playing at hide-and-seek in and out of their hidden doorways.

Cropear was lying on the ground stretched out on his stomach and resting on his elbows, his chin in his palms. He

38

suddenly became aware of the dull *tlot, tlot* of an approaching broncho. This was not strange, for he had often met ponies. But now he became conscious of a strange odor. Cropear prided himself on knowing every scent of every animal in his part of the world. This, however, was different; it tickled his nose and was like fire in the wild grasses. It was, in fact, the first whiff of tobacco he had smelled since he was a child, and it awakened in him a vague memory of a world of long lost dreams.

Immediately Cropear became curious and forgot for the moment the first and most universal law of the Pack—the law of staying put, of sitting so still that he could not be seen. He sat up suddenly and threw his head about to see what this strange smell might be. There, but a few yards distant, the buckskin cow pony and his rider, Chuck, came to a sudden, slithering halt.

Cropear suddenly let out three scared yelps and turned on his heels to run away. Chuck—himself a perfect mimic—repeated the scared yelps. This aroused Cropear's curiosity further. He stopped and let out another series of yelps. These Chuck again repeated. In the Coyote language, Cropear was asking, "Who are you? Who are you?" Chuck was repeating this question without in the least knowing what the yips meant.

Thus began the most amusing dialogue in all the history of talk. Cropear would bark a question over and over, and in reply Chuck would mimic him perfectly.

Cropear kept galloping in circles, curiously sniffing, and wondering when and where it was he had smelled man and tobacco. Chuck kept his hand on his gun and his eyes on the strange wild creature. He couldn't help admiring the sheer physical beauty of this perfect, healthy wild man. Every muscle was so fully developed that he looked like another Hercules.

Cropear was, in fact, as straight as a wagon-tongue. His skin, from living all his life in the open sunlight and wind, was a lustrous brown, covered with a fine silken fell of burnished red hair. Over his shoulders lay the bristling mane of his unshorn locks.

After an hour or two of galloping about, Cropear lost much of his fear, approached nearer, and squatted down on his haunches to see what would happen.

"You're a funny baby!" Chuck laughed.

"Funny baby," Cropear lisped like a child of four.

The cowpuncher talked in a low, musical accent; and slowly and brokenly at first, Cropear began to prattle. He was taking up the thread of his speech where he had dropped it years before when he was lost by his family.

For nearly a month Chuck wandered around on the mesa and continued his dialogue with Cropear. Chuck would patiently repeat words and sentences many times. He was forced to use his hands and arms and his face and voice to illustrate all that he said. But Cropear proved such an apt pupil that soon he was saying and understanding everything. What's more, Cropear's speech became far more grammatical than Chuck's own, for only the finest language had ever been permitted among the Coyotes. And Cropear had evolved a combination of the two. The worst he ever said from then on, in cowboy lingo, was just an ain't or two.

Chuck was astonished at the speed with which he learned. "He's brighter'n a new minted dollar!" Chuck declared to his broncho.

Over and over Chuck asked Cropear, "Who in the name of common sense are you, anyhow?" Cropear tried his best to remember, yet all he knew was that he was a Coyote. "But who are you?" Cropear asked in turn.

"My real name is Bob Hunt," Chuck laughed, "but the boys all call me Chuckwagon because I'm always hungry—Chuck for short." He drawled his words musically as he swung into an easy position across his saddle. "What are you doin', runnin' around here naked like a wild Coyote, that's what I want to know?"

"I *am* a Coyote," Cropear snapped back.

"Coyote, nothin'! You're a *human!*"

"An accursed *human!* I guess not! I wouldn't belong to that degraded *inhuman* race for anything in the world. Haven't I got fleas? Don't I hunt with the pack and run the fleet prong-horn Antelope and the spry Jack-rabbit off their legs? And don't I sit on my haunches, and don't I have my place in the circle, and don't I howl at night in accordance with the ancient approved custom of all thoroughbred Coyotes? Don't you suppose I know who I am as well as you?" Cropear answered quite out of patience.

"You've just been eatin' of the locoweed and are a little out of your head," laughed Chuck. "Besides, every human in Texas has got fleas, so that's got nothin' at all to do with it."

"I haven't been eating of the locoweed! Only silly cattle and mustangs do a thing like that. I *am* in my right mind—and what's more, I *am* a Coyote!"

"You're loco, or else I am," insisted the smiling Chuck. "Why, you're a *human* just the same as I am. Don't you know that every Coyote's got a long bushy tail? Now, you ain't got no tail at all and you know it."

Strange as it may seem, this was the first time that Cropear had really looked himself over, and sure enough, he saw at once that he had no tail.

"But no one has ever before said that to me. Perhaps—no, I won't believe it. I don't want to be a depraved *inhuman.* . . . I know, for all you say, that I'm a full-blooded noble Coyote!"

Because of his sudden fears, Cropear was fighting to hold to his belief.

"If you wasn't so perfectly serious about it all, you'd be a downright scream," Chuck cackled. "As it is, I almost pity you."

"You're the one who needs to be pitied," snarled Cropear. "Anyone that's got to be an *inhuman* needs pity. Here you sit with a piece of cowhide over your head, the wool of the sheep over your shoulders and legs, and calfskin over your feet. Why, you can't even use your own legs. You've got to have a broncho to carry you around fast. Me, an *inhuman* human, no!" Cropear fairly spat his words, he was so disgusted.

"Human!" Chuck continued. *"Human!* Why, say, you're the only perfect human critter I've ever laid eyes on. If I had the muscles you've got, I'd turn in some mornin' before breakfast and beat up every prize fighter in all creation, and that within an inch of his life."

"But you haven't yet proved I'm not a noble Coyote," Cropear added with stubborn courage.

"It's proof you want, is it? Well, then, come with me and I'll give you all the proof you'll ever need, and that in a hurry."

Chuck swung his idle foot into the stirrup, spun his pony around like a top, and struck out in the direction of the Pecos River. At first he walked his broncho, but Cropear trotting along in front of him, set a faster stride. Next he paced his pony, but still Cropear ran far ahead and beckoned him to follow. Soon he was galloping at full tilt. The broncho was doing its best, but Cropear idled along at a graceful lope that seemed easier than walking. Chuck rubbed his eyes and could not believe that Cropear could run so far and so fast.

When they arrived at the river, Chuck led Cropear down to the water's edge. Here he found a quiet pool beside the racing current, where the reflection made a perfect mirror.

"Wade in a bit. There, stand still, lean over and look at yourself," Chuck commanded.

While Cropear was leaning over the water without an idea in the world that he was looking at himself, Chuck began to kick off his clothes. "Look at what you see down below there," he called. "Ain't we as alike as two mustangs from the same herd?"

Cropear obeyed. There, in the water, he saw a creature who looked like Chuck—but didn't. What was it? Cropear moved his head to the left, and the creature's head moved in the same direction. He moved to the right. The creature moved the other way.

Was Chuck right, then? It was an appalling thought. That he was an *inhuman,* after all, was so terrible to Cropear, he was without words for reply. For a long moment, he stood silent and motionless. Then he looked down at his reflection again. Surely this was all a bad dream!

Now Chuck waded in and threw his arm around the sorrowful boy's shoulder. "Come on down," he said, pulling Cropear in beside him. "Now look. Here I am and there you are."

Without a doubt, there was Chuck's reflection. And there,

beside him, must be Cropear, the coyote. An *inhuman!*
Nothing could possibly be worse.

Just at this instant, Chuck caught sight of a strange mark
on Cropear's upper right arm—a tattooed star, showing plainly
through the red fell of hair.

"I'll be locoed if I ain't got one of them, too," he cried,
pointing to a similar mark on his own arm.

Cropear looked first at his arm, then at Chuck's. "What
does it mean?" he asked, slowly.

"It means you're found. You're my little lost brother Bill.
You ain't Cropear and you ain't never been."

Cropear stood stone still. "Your brother?"

"Surest thing you know. Listen. This is how I know.
When Dad was travelin' around once with a Patent Medicine
Man, he learned how to do this here tattooin'. So when us
kids arrived, Mother got the idea it'd be a good thing to have
a big star on the arm of each and every one of us. She said
she didn't intend any of us ever to forget the Lone Star State
we belonged to. And what's more, if any one of us happened
to get lost, this star would help find us. So, as usual, Mother
was right! You got lost but you're found again. See?"

"Now you sound as if you're the one that's been eating of
the locoweed and gone crazy," Cropear replied.

"It's the honest truth, I'm tellin' you. I'd be willin' to stand
on a stack of Bibles as high as the moon and repeat every
word of it out in public, if you'd but quit your foolish notion
that you're a varmint."

"Varmint, indeed!" Cropear snarled. "You're completely
locoed. It's the pale-faced *inhumans* that are low-down varmints! Coyotes are the noblest of all the earth's creatures!"

Fortunately Chuck was so interested in the story he was

*Because an immigrant settles thirty-five miles away, Pecos Bill's
mother decides to move*

just beginning that he did not take time to answer this last insult.

"Honestly, Cropear—Bill, I mean. This is what happened. Our family was goin' along from the Brazos River valley down to the Rio Grande. Dad was drivin' a little east Texas spotted cow and a little wall-eyed spavined roan horse. They was hitched to an old covered wagon with wooden wheels made from cross sections of a sycamore tree. Mother'd insisted it was gettin' too crowded up there in Texas, and she wanted to be where there was at least elbow room."

"Your mother must have had a wide sweep of elbows," Cropear commented.

"Yes, we lived a hundred miles from the nearest town and seventy-five miles from the nearest tradin' post. But an immigrant settled down thirty-five miles away, and Mother said we'd got to move. She couldn't have any stranger settlin' in her back yard, she said."

"What kind of woman was she, anyway?" Cropear asked curiously.

"Well, judge for yourself. She swept forty-five Indian Chiefs out of her back yard with her broomstick one mornin' before breakfast. You see, she found them prowlin' around, set on doin' mischief, and she sent them flyin' with one swoop and never give it more never mind than as if they was a bunch of sage chickens, or meddlesome porcupines.

"You probably don't remember it, but you cut your teeth on a Bowie knife that Davy Crockett sent our mother as a present when he heard what a brave, wise woman she was."

"Well, that's the kind of mother I have always dreamed I would like. Perhaps I am partly *human*, after all," Cropear now conceded. This mother sounded very fine indeed!

"Well, as we was migratin' in the covered wagon," Chuck continued without noticing the remark, "I guess you jumped overboard right along about here. Half a day passed before the rest of us discovered that you was missin', and then when we come back, we couldn't find you."

"My mother must have loved me dearly!" Cropear snarled, bitterly resentful that he could have meant as little to so splendid a person. "Not missing me for half a day! Nothing like that ever happened between me and Grandy. Why, he loved me so he never allowed me out of his sight for a single minute, day or night!"

"You don't get the idea at all," Chuck continued. "You see, it was like this. You had eighteen brothers and sisters, more or less. Well, after you was lost overboard, there was still seventeen of us flounderin' around in the covered wagon. One more or less didn't make no difference. Besides, there was one younger than you was—Henrietta—and she was mewlin' and droolin' in your dear mother's arms up on the front seat beside your father, the whole of the way. Your older sister, Sophrina, was supposed to look after you, but she got to quarrelin' with brother Hoke. He was teasin' her about her best beau, that had been left behind on the Brazos, at the edge of our thirty-five-mile back yard. So it was perfectly natural for you to jump overboard when no one was lookin', and then not be missed for a long time."

"So that was it," Cropear said as in a dream. "But when my mother discovered that I was gone, what then?"

"Well, it was the old story of the 'Ninety and Nine' all over again each day, ever after. Your mother had the whole seventeen of us to feed and look after; but she was often talkin' about her Little Lost Bill. Sometimes she put in the

Pecos part, for the last sight she had of you was when she inspected things just before the wagon started to ford this river. She used to wake up in the middle of the night and get to thinkin' the Coyotes and Grizzly Bears was crunchin' your tender bones. And I can hear her yet, at table, sighin' as she looked at your vacant chair. Her last words when she died were, 'Now I'll be seein' Little Bill!' "

"The dear good woman," Cropear sighed, in genuine relief, "but I can never love her as I love Grandy. And what about my father?"

Chuck laughed loud and long. "He was a regular copperas breeches and one gallus kind of man. He had seven dogs, a cob pipe and a roll of home-spun tobacco stuck down his pocket. He would spend more time pokin' a rabbit out of a hollow tree than he would to secure shelter for his family in a storm. He could easily afford to have one or two of his children blow away, but rabbits was too scarce to take the chance of losin' one! You see, he didn't count for much with Mother. A woman who could sweep out forty-five big Indian Chiefs with a single broom-handle couldn't be expected to show much mercy for a mere husband.

"Besides, she'd never have been able to scare the Big Chiefs so easily if she hadn't been practisin' up on her own old man! Fact is, she was the cock of the walk at our ranch. Dad merely took orders. We nicknamed him Moses. But Mother was the God of the Mountain! She wrote her commands on tables of stone and the poor man who received them from her hands was meek. I'm tellin' you, he was meek!"

"Your story begins to sound reasonable, and I do agree that I now see a faint likeness between us. . . . But I don't want to be an *inhuman!* I don't want to have to wear clothes and ride horses. I want to be free! I want to continue to be strong. I want to be healthy like my brothers, the Bears, the Wolves, and the Coyotes, who are wild and natural and vigorous! I want to live where I can lay me down on a sheet of mist and roll up in a blanket of fog. I want to sleep where I can breathe the clean air and see the countless eyes of all my brother animals peeping down at me as they race across the sky!"

"Don't be a fool, brother. It's high time for you to forget that you was ever called Cropear. It's right and proper for you now to become Pecos Bill. Come with me and I'll take you to the ranch house, where you'll be happier than you've ever been yet."

"But I can't think of going with you today. I've at least got to go back and take my farewell of the Pack."

"Well then, tomorrow. Tomorrow I'll come for you. And I'll say we'll teach you the gentlest of all ancient arts, the art of the ranch. Oh yes, you'll still be right in the great out-of-doors. With your strength like an ox and your spry heels, you'll become the greatest of all the great cowmen the world has ever known."

Chuck's words stirred something deep within Cropear's nature. What it was, he did not know. But he saw clearly in this instant, that come what might, he must go with Chuck. Lifting his head with a gesture of determination, he said solemnly, "Brother Chuck, I hear the call! Today I bid you adieu; tomorrow I join you!"

With these words and without once looking back, Cropear loped easily over the chappiro, across the rolling mesa. He skirted the sage brush and was soon lost in the haze of the distant mesquite.

Chuck rubbed his eyes for a moment to make certain that this was something more than a day dream. Then he pulled on his high-heeled boots, tightened his jingling spurs, swung aboard his astonished buckskin pony and was off. All the way home to the ranch house he sang so loud that he fairly cracked his voice:

"With my seat in the sky and my knees in the saddle,
I'm going to teach Pecos Bill to punch Texas cattle.
　　Get along, little dogies, get along, get along;
　　Get along, little dogies, get along.
　　Coma ti yi youpy, youpy ya!
　　Coma ti yi youpy, youpy ya!"

III.

PECOS BILL MEETS A COWPUNCHER

When Chuck reached the ranch house he was still loudly singing with a sharp nasal twang:

"Coma ti yi youpy, youpy ya!"

"Where've you been all this time and what's happened to you now, Chuck?" drawled Legs, his best pal, who was sitting on the back steps waiting for supper. "I've always said the world would sure come to an evil end when either you or the wild Indians turned musical. You sound like a cross between a blackbird and a kingfisher."

"Well, if you'd been where I've been, and if you'd seen what I've seen, you'd be musical, too! I just keep singin' along to prove to myself that I'm not loco!" answered Chuck as he swung down from the saddle.

"You don't say," said Legs curiously.

"Yes, I've just come from down across the Pecos where I met a *human* who thinks he's a Coyote! He's runnin' around down there with no clothes like a regular varmint. He's got enough red hair down the back of his neck to braid a rope a mile long. And the sagebrush on his face and chest would cover half the ranch. Yes, and he's prattlin' about what noble creatures the Coyotes are, and what low-down, depraved degenerates we *inhumans* are!" As he spoke, Chuck sat down.

"You don't mean it," Legs laughed and slapped his boot with his open palm in glee.

"When I told him he was a *human,* he said that couldn't possibly be true, because he said he had got fleas same as all other Coyotes!"

"We're Coyotes then, too, you bet!" Legs laughed.

"Then I tried to convince him that he'd got no tail and so he couldn't possibly be a Coyote. Well, after a while I was able to show him that he looked more like me than he looked like his whole pack of varmints put together. Yes, and you won't believe me when I tell you that he easily outran the best I could do on Old Pepper for more'n ten miles. He can run antelope and jack-rabbits off their feet, and there's no mistake about it. I saw him do it with my own two eyes, I'm tellin' you."

"Guess I best get my gun, Chuck, and take you out to the place for locoed cayuses. You're as crazy as a frothin' steer!" drawled Legs.

"Yes, and listen to this," Chuck continued without noticing the remark. "This *human's* got a tattooed star on his forearm just like this one I wear here. It looks to me as if he's my brother, Pecos Bill, the one I told you that got lost overboard when the folks was movin' us children to the Rio Grande. The fact seems to be that the Coyotes have reared this lost brother of mine as a loyal member of their pack, and that they've made him believe all these years that he's a full-blooded Coyote himself. Yes, and what's more, they've taught him to hate us *inhumans* worse than if we was bad-blooded rattlesnakes."

"Well," grinned Legs, "congratulations. You get loonier and loonier. You're locoed all right. Wait a minute till I fetch my gun, before you begin to froth at the mouth and get dangerous."

"Tomorrow mornin'," said Chuck seriously, "I'm goin' to take an extra broncho and some of my clothes and go down to the river and tow him back here to the ranch. Then you'll very soon see that you'll be just as locoed about him as I am. And if everything don't turn out just like I'm tellin' you, then I'll eat your lead."

Two hours later as the men of the ranch squatted round their gypsy fire, eating their evening meal, Chuck related his experience to them.

At first they all declared that Chuck should be shot for trying to make them believe such a yarn. But when he seemed to them a bit too anxious to bet them everything he owned, even to his buckskin shirt and his Mexican saddle and Old Pepper, his broncho pony, they weren't so sure.

"Well, if it's as you say," said Gun Smith, the natural leader of the outfit, "we're goin' to have a regular circus when the noble son of a Coyote arrives. By the time we have initiated him into the sacred rites of the Ancient and Renowned Order of the Knights of the Round Table of the Genus Bovine, the Cowpuncher, he'll know at least one thing, I'm tellin' you. He'll never forget that a Human is a Human and that a Coyote is a Coyote!"

The others were in cordial agreement. "We'll soon pound all the Coyote ideas out of his head!" they shouted.

"I move that we make Gun Smith the Master of Ceremonies," announced Fat Adams.

"Agreed," called everybody in a hearty chorus.

"What you tell the greenhorn Coyote to do, we'll see that he does it, and that promptly, or our names is not the Boys of the I. X. L. Ranch!" pledged a dozen voices.

"I don't care much what you do to him," drawled Chuck with serious face. "Only, please remember he's my baby brother. Don't you go shootin' him or breakin' any of his bones. And remember this, he'll likely turn out a pretty stubborn cayuse before you've got him goin'. Believe me, he's nobody's fool. He learns things quicker'n anybody I've ever seen."

"I foresee we're goin' to have a very warm evenin' as soon as he arrives," chuckled Gun Smith.

"In fact, he looks to me like the smartest of the whole Hunt family," Chuck added dreamily.

Thus it was agreed that Pecos Bill should receive everything in their bag of tricks when it came to giving him the customary initiation of a greenhorn entering the cow camp.

The following morning when Chuck guided Old Pepper and the trailing pony across the river at the ford, he found Pecos Bill sitting on his haunches, waiting. Pecos had just finished putting on an old, ill-fitting man's suit, and he was more uncomfortable than he had ever been before in his life.

At first Chuck could scarcely believe his eyes. When he did fully recognize his brother, he let out a hearty laugh.

"You didn't pick 'em quite soon enough," he grinned broadly.

"I don't understand at all what you mean," Pecos answered.

"You left 'em on the bush two or three months too long. ... Your clothes, I mean. They're a mile and a half too big for you. What were you tryin' to do when you bought them —get your money's worth?"

"I didn't buy them," Pecos answered, feeling very upset that his brother did not like his clothes. "They were given to me!"

"And who, may I ask, handed 'em down to you?"

"The Coyote pack. My brothers, of course. We all knew that it wouldn't be quite right for me to go with you to the ranch house without anything on, and so the Coyotes stripped these off the body of a cowboy who was killed in a fight last night, far over the mesa."

"I'll have to tell you," Chuck replied very seriously, "that you're makin' a terrible bad mistake. It ain't considered good manners, Pecos, to be found wearin' the clothes some other man has died in."

Then, to make sure that Pecos was not trying to fool him, Chuck swung easily down from Old Pepper and made a personal examination. Sure enough, there was the bullet hole and the blood stain, and the numerous teeth marks of the Coyotes. After a few seconds, Chuck added, "Pecos, you had best take 'em off right away!"

"Strange," thought Pecos to himself, "that these *humans* are so careful not to wear the clothes of a dead man, when all the while they wear clothes made of dead animals."

Now Chuck sauntered easily over to where Old Pepper was nibbling the bunch grass and untied a neat bundle from behind his saddlebags: "Here, brother Pecos, try these."

Pecos was much perplexed. But he struggled out of the dead man's suit and picked up the clothes Chuck had brought him.

"You're as awkward, Pecos, as the noodle that hung his trousers high on a peg and then tried to take a runnin' start and jump into them," Chuck commented. "Here, take hold of the top this way."

After Pecos had succeeded in wriggling into his clothes, Chuck stood back and admired him: "Why, you'll be handsomer than General George Washington, brother Pecos, when you get some of the bristlin' sagebrush off your neck and that autumn tinged bunch grass off your cheeks and chin."

"What a strange race these *humans* are," thought Pecos again to himself. "They seem to delight most of all in undoing everything that Mother Nature has done so well for them."

Pecos knew that although he was rapidly learning a great deal, he was still far from being the man his brother was. And he felt shy and bashful.

"Here, Pecos, stand still," Chuck was now saying, as he got out a sizable pair of scissors. "I got a job to do. You can't go ridin' up to the ranch with such a nestin' place for the varmints around your neck and ears."

"But I thought you said yesterday that all *humans* had fleas," Pecos objected nervously.

"The only difference," crooned Chuck, "is that the Coyotes

have got a few more fleas according to size than the humans."

As he talked, Chuck's shears moved rapidly and great shocks of red hair fell to the ground. "It'll take only another minute to crop off a couple o' yards of your mane with these warranted broncho shears," Chuck rattled on. "There, that's a thousand per cent better already. Yes, and now we'll just waltz up and down your cheeks a few times for good measure. Why, you can just hear the fleas howl as the shears overtake 'em. Never mind, you're beginnin' to look somethin' like yourself now. By the little roan bull's bellow, you're as perfect as old Davy Crockett, and the world will bear me out in that statement as soon as she's been properly introduced."

Chuck stopped to admire his handiwork.

"Man alive," he continued musically, "you're the first brother o' mine I've ever seen that I'm proud to call my own. Let me tell you, you put to shame every other human of the whole Southwest Empire, or I'm a liar."

After he had worked half an hour longer trimming and brushing his brother, Chuck began to think of the ranch house. "Well, brother Pecos, now that you're lookin' so fine, we had best be ridin' along."

Pecos started to walk over to the waiting ponies, but his gait resembled nothing so much as a kitten with paper tied to its feet.

"These boots! They're terrible," he groaned. "My feet, oh, my feet! Please, Brother Chuck, let me wear the boots my brother Coyotes gave me."

"Now, my boy," Chuck smiled kindly, "a cowpuncher's feet has got to be as small almost as the feet of a woman."

Pecos mournfully squatted on his haunches to relieve the pain. "Feet like a woman!" he groaned.

Pecos Bill gets his first haircut

Chuck was firm. "You've got to make up your mind to it. That's all. Cowboy does as cowboy does, my lad."

"Is it as bad as that?" Pecos sighed under his breath. "Is there no freedom among *humans?* Why, even the wild Coyote pack allows some choice."

"I see clearly enough," Chuck smiled as he observed how impossible it was for Pecos to walk, "I see that you'll have to wear the dead man's boots. . . . But never breathe a word about where you got 'em, for if the I. X. L. Outfit ever gets on to it, they'll be on your neck."

"Worse and more of it!" Pecos moaned.

"Your feet has been out to pasture too long for their own good," Chuck continued with a kindly grin. "But after you keep 'em in the corral for a month of Sundays or longer, they'll shrink down just like the sides of a fat steer in winter, or pork that's killed in the decrease of the moon."

So Pecos changed his boots and the reunited brothers started on their way.

As their ponies cantered along toward the ranch house of the I. X. L. Outfit the thought that most agitated Pecos Bill was his strengthened conviction that all human beings—with the exception, perhaps, of his brother Chuck—were depraved *inhumans.* They must be, if Chuck was as afraid of them as he seemed. Why shouldn't a person wear dead men's boots?

IV.

PECOS BILL BECOMES A COWPUNCHER

When Chuck arrived at the ranch house with Pecos Bill, the bronzed cowpunchers were squatting on their heels in an irregular circle about their open gypsy fire. Their tin plates were piled high with hunks of their favorite boiled cow and potatoes and frying pan bread. Violent black coffee was steaming in their tin cups.

Chuck began by introducing his brother: "Gun Smith, this is Pecos Bill. Pecos, this is Fat Adams. This is Mushmouth.

And this is Bullfrog Doyle. This is Moon Hennessey. Pretty Pete Rogers, meet my brother, Pecos. Bean Hole—"

"It's a funny way they have of naming one another," thought Pecos as his sharp eyes caught a vivid picture of each. Gun Smith had a great Colt cannon—a revolver—dangling from each side of his belt, with a third gun thrust into the open bosom of his shirt. Fat Adams was so lean and tall that he didn't even cast a shadow when he stood sideways to the sun. Mushmouth had a lip piano—his mouth organ—in each breast pocket. He was as lean and large jointed as a hungry Timber Wolf. Bullfrog Doyle, whose feet kept moving about as if he were tap dancing, reminded Pecos of a nervous Prairie Dog.

Moon Hennessey had a mouth as big as the Pecos River, and looked as if he could drink the ocean dry, if necessary. Legs was a squatty, bow-legged creature, whose shanks were so short that he could walk half a day within the circle of an ordinary calf noose without reaching the edge. Pretty Pete Rogers was a dandy. He was as proud and sleek as a Peacock and had his ten-gallon hat and belt ornamented with a hundred silver cartwheels, better known as dollars. And Bean Hole, the cook, was as fat as a butter firkin.

While Chuck was still in the act of introducing Pecos Bill, the men all suddenly jumped to their feet and ran away, pell-mell, leaving their food behind them. At a safe distance they turned about, with hands on guns, and began talking loudly for Pecos Bill's benefit.

"What kind of varmint is it?" they exclaimed, pointing at Pecos.

"It can't be a Coyote, for it ain't got a tail like a Coyote!"

"It ain't a Giraffe either. Its neck ain't long enough!"

"If it was a Mountain Lion, its growl would be louder!"

"It ain't got quite nasty enough eyes for a Wouser!"

"It looks mighty dangerous, though, whatever it is!"

"It sure does!"

"Do you really suppose it's got the hydrophobia?"

"Say, did you ever see a critter in your life look so down-right vicious?"

Then with a show of extreme caution, the men returned, but nervously and on tip-toe. One by one they took up their plates and again began to eat. All the while they looked suspiciously out of the corner of their eyes at Pecos Bill, as if ready to run should he make the slightest move.

Pecos Bill entirely missed the point. "These *humans,* after all, aren't so different from the Coyotes," he was saying to himself. "They have just as much caution as the wild animals."

The cowpunchers were enormously elated, for they thought their deception was successful, and that Pecos Bill actually was believing that they were scared out of their wits.

Next, Chuck motioned Pecos to a place within the irregular circle and Bean Hole brought him a plate stacked with victuals. The men were all watching him like cats watch a mouse to see how he would eat.

Now the clever Coyotes had taught Pecos a lesson which at this moment served him well. "Always look before you leap," Grandy had yipped a thousand times into Pecos Bill's ears.

So Pecos had looked and had quickly seen that the cowboy custom had decreed that the knife of the cowboy must go into the mouth with every bite of food. He also saw that no time was allowed for talk while the meal was in progress.

Trying to use a knife was at first awkward and clumsy for

Pecos Bill, and he lost his first and second bites on the ground between his legs. He even hit his nose once or twice instead of his mouth. But after some effort he learned to spear the chunks of meat in the very center, and to shovel the grub stake as fast as anybody. Pecos Bill was, in fact, so bent on making a good first impression that he never once thought to notice how flat the cooked food tasted.

As soon as Gun Smith had finished eating, he got up leisurely and began sauntering carelessly around the circle. He rolled a cigarette in one hand with cool unconcern. He lighted his match with a quick flip of his thumb nail. Then he threw a tomato can into the air, drew his gun from his breast with perfect ease, and put a hole through the very center of the flying tin. Next he cracked off the neck of a flying bottle, and finally he put a hole through the center of a small coin which he had thrown so that it would alight in the plate from which Pecos was eating.

All the while he was silently studying the impression he was making on Pecos Bill. Chuck had done such a good job of clearing away the bunch grass and the sagebrush from his brother's face that Pecos looked quite like a human. And the men all suspected that Pecos was a seasoned cowboy, and that Chuck and his brother were putting up a job on them.

The clothes were Chuck's, they saw. But the boots? Would a human, who believed himself to be a Coyote, be wearing a pair of regular cowboy boots? And where did the boots come from? They were not Chuck's. Then there was the nasty looking butt of a Colt's revolver protruding from its holster. This belt and gun had never belonged to Chuck either. What would a Coyote be doing with a gun? They cast suspicious glances at each other with each new discovery.

The men were immensely fascinated with Pecos Bill's finely set-up figure. It was closely knit and perfect in every detail. And they were even more charmed with the bronzed features and the deep, clear eyes. And each was secretly aware of a strange power in Pecos which was something naturally to be feared. They were aware, too, that the stranger was not quite able to hide the fact that he was seeing everything for the first time and that he was intensely interested and even surprised in all that he observed. There was more to this brother of Chuck's than they had thought.

But they wouldn't let him know how they felt. Certainly not! So Gun Smith asked carelessly, "What do you say to practisin' a little shootin', Pecos?"

"I'd like to be excused, if you please," Pecos replied, not a little surprised by this sudden question.

"Why? Ain't your gun workin' this evenin'?" Gun Smith smiled with a shrug of his shoulders.

"No, it's not working just now," Pecos answered.

"Perhaps you'd like to borrow my gun?"

"No, thank you, at least not tonight."

"Then, perhaps you'd let me examine your gun. Like as not I can put it in workin' order for you," Gun Smith persisted.

"Is this a cowboy custom?" Pecos asked innocently as he appealed to his brother Chuck.

"Why, yes and no," Chuck answered quietly, not wishing to be drawn into the affair. "It's just as you like either way."

"Well, I'll leave the gun where it is then," Pecos said.

Gun Smith rolled another cigarette with the cool poise of a royal prince, and as he did so, he strolled about and inquired silently from the eyes of the others what he should do next.

The signal that shot from eye to eye was to proceed with

whatever in his judgment was best. Gun Smith noticed the falling shadows of night and was happy.

"Well," he sighed, "since you don't care to waste your lead on tin and glass, wouldn't you like to go out gunnin' for real game? You see, there's a terrible monster of a Wouser down the canyon a ways. He's already carried off a dozen of our four-year-old steers. And last night he begun to show his man-eatin' tendencies by carryin' off Cayenne Joe, spurs, gun and all. What would you say to guardin' the main trail while I go up above and drive this terrible Wouser down for you to shoot?"

"Since you're such a fine marksman, and since I'm especially spry on my legs, I think I prefer to do the driving myself," replied Pecos quickly, as he leapt to his feet.

There was an instant interchange of thought in the flashing eyes of the men as much as to say, "What's this? This Pecos ain't no Coyote greenhorn."

"You'd best let me stick to the drivin', Pecos. I know every foot of the land hereabouts and we can get the job over sooner with me doin' it. You see, we eat only humans for breakfast each mornin' in this outfit," Gun Smith declared with a straight face. "One carcass lasts us anywheres from seven weeks to two months. This mornin' we begun on the last pickled piece of Podgy Ike. We're just naturally so lazy we prefer to eat one another rather than be bothered with goin' out and wagin' a war with neighbor ranchers in order to pick off one of their mangy cow-hands. For the one that's next in greasin' Bean Hole's frying pan, we draw lots. Whoever happens to pull the lucky card goes out and asks Bean Hole please to chop off his infernal head and serve him up in steak for the next breakfast."

Pecos Bill listened respectfully.

"There's one thing you've forgot," chirped Legs now with a great show of seriousness. "Pecos Bill's a stranger, and besides, he's not a legal member of our outfit. He ain't exactly obligated to take part in our lottery under these conditions, is he?"

"Thank you," Gun Smith smiled good-naturedly. "But we can set that right in short order. How about it, Pecos? How about joinin' our I. X. L. outfit? Then you'll be eligible for our lottery."

Once more Grandy's caution came to the fore. "I've not exactly decided what I want to do," Pecos replied, without at all understanding the trick they were playing on him.

"But you see," Gun Smith continued, "we're beginnin' to feel a strong likin' for you already. You're modest, and you're healthy and you'd make an excellent broth. Besides, we need you to help fill in our thinnin' ranks. What do you say, fellows, what do you say? I move we vote Pecos Bill into our outfit to take the place of Cayenne Joe, who was murdered by the Wouser yesterday."

"We'll just see a show of hands," shouted Legs.

Every hand except that of Pecos shot up.

"I'm happy to tell you, Pecos Bill, that you're unanimously elected."

It was now dark, and there came from the outside of the ranch a yowl louder than twenty Lions and fifty Bobcats could have made if they had all joined in a single chorus. It was Mushmouth, in what his friends considered his most talented role.

"Well, Pecos," Gun Smith urged, "we'd best be settin' out on our hunt. You hear for yourself the roarin' Wouser, and

besides, we want to get the job finished off before time for
the lottery to begin."

"That was not the language of a Wouser," said Pecos Bill
coolly. "I know the language of every living creature of this
country, and can talk to each animal in his own tongue. That
noise sounded exactly like a very bad imitation of what a
human thinks a Wouser should sound like. This is what a
Wouser says when he sounds the blood call: 'Gr-gr-gr-Wouw-
ow-ow! Wouw-ow-ow-ow-ow! Gr-gr-gr-gr-gr-gr! Wouw-
ow-wow-ow-ow!' "

It was a shrill, murderous scream, repeated a dozen times
with growing intensity. It rent the silence to tatters and curdled the blood. The men started from their places and pulled
their guns.

"Wait a minute," said Pecos, before anyone could speak,
"I'll just gallop down through the canyon, and if there's a
Wouser within sound of my voice, I'll be talking with him
across the mesquite inside of a minute; and if you want me
to, I'll bring him back with me—alive."

Everyone was too frightened to speak until Pecos was gone.
Then the men fell upon Chuck in a rage.

"A nice greenhorn, your Pecos is," they shouted together.
"He's an old timer disguised as the son of a Coyote. You've
brought him here to make fools of us!"

"What I've told you is true, every word of it," Chuck pro-
tested. "No ordinary *human* could give such a blood-curdlin'
yell like that. Why, the best Mushmouth could do sounded
like a Katydid compared to a Grizzly Bear. Besides, the reason he didn't want to use his gun is because he don't know
how. I know where the boots and the gun come from. And
neither Pecos nor me is to blame for this, either."

"You're a cheerful liar."

Chuck grinned. "You just wait and see."

In the silence that ensued there was a quick series of echoing yells, more blood-curdling even than the first the men had heard. They came from far off, down by the mouth of the canyon, upward of a mile distant.

"What's that?" the men asked each other nervously.

"That's brother Pecos," Chuck smiled. "I'm telling you, he can split the wind three times as fast as a bald eagle. In a minute he'll be back again."

With this, Mushmouth came racing back into the circle by the open fire, his face as white as a sheet. "Who's this two-heeled demon you fetched here, Chuck? One minute he scares the daylights out of us inside the circle. The next, he kicks off his boots like greased lightnin' and flies off faster'n a bullet. And then you hear that infernal Wouser cry! He's locoed, that's what. And we'll never be able to find our ponies or our steers after such goin's-on as this. They're out there now snortin' and pawin' up the turf like locoed cayuses, all because of that infernal yowlin'."

"Well," drawled Gun Smith, "since I'm the director of this little show, what's to be the next turn on the program? Most of the things we'd planned can't be put across with this son of the Coyotes."

"I advise you to have the cards shuffled and ready for the lottery. Pecos'll be back any minute," Chuck added.

Again a series of blood-curdling yells came distinctly to the ears of the scared cowboys. This time they were another mile farther up the canyon.

"What I've told you is the whole truth, and nothin' but the truth," persisted Chuck. "Watch out—here he comes!"

Sure enough, within five minutes Pecos came leaping back into the circle as spry as a kitten and in such a hurry to get back he had entirely forgotten to put his boots back on. When the men saw his feet, they were quite willing to believe anything. The callouses were like those on the soles of wild beasts and the toes were hairy and clawed like a Coyote's.

"You're quite mistaken about the Wouser," Pecos Bill began promptly. "I gave his call of blood twice—once at either end of the canyon. If he had been anywhere near, he would have answered. Besides, I talked with two different Coyotes, and they told me that there isn't a single Wouser within a hundred miles of here. The Coyotes know everything that is happening in all directions up and down the mesa, you all know that."

"Spoken with a Coyote," scoffed Gun Smith. "Which reminds me—one or the other of us will soon be talkin' with St. Peter! It's time now to start the lottery. We can't be without decent food for breakfast, you know."

There was a great show of shuffling the cards. Legs made his hand fairly fly. Then when he thought Pecos wouldn't see, he substituted a deck which was already stacked.

"Does the low card win tonight as usual?" asked Legs with a pretense of honesty, when the cards were ready.

"That's for you all to decide," purred Gun Smith innocently.

"I move we make it the high card for a change—the King high, Ace low," challenged Mushmouth.

"All in favor show your claws!" Gun Smith directed, looking sharply at Pecos.

Instantly a dozen hands flew into the air like drawn pistols.

"The high card wins," announced Gun Smith.

When the drawing was complete, Pecos Bill held the fated high card.

"Just run along now and ask Bean Hole to cut off your head and quarter you and souse what we don't need of you for breakfast into the meat barrel," Gun Smith commanded with pretended deep sadness.

"What are you trying to make me believe, anyhow?" Pecos grinned. "I've just taken a whiff of your meat barrel and there's never been anything in it but *Cow!*"

It was a complete victory for Pecos Bill.

Before the men could stop laughing at Gun Smith's failure, Pecos asked if he might not entertain them with the toe dance of the pack. "Whenever a great honor befalls a Coyote, he is asked to dance."

"You sure can!" shouted a dozen amused voices.

With this, Pecos Bill led the still half-suspicious cowboys out into the open away from the glare of the fire. Here on a level piece of turf he began to leap slowly at first, then with rapidly increasing speed, until no one was quite certain that he saw Pecos at all.

First Pecos turned the small circle and then the reverse circle; then the figure eight, then the reverse figure eight. He flopped forward and then backward; he turned cartwheels and reverse cartwheels. He rolled nimbly back and forth on the ground, all the while giving the lonely mournful yip and howl of the wild Coyote.

The men were fascinated and were immediately sure that Pecos was the greatest magician of all time. Suddenly stopping in his tracks, he assumed the rigid pose of invisibility that Grandy had taught him, and asked the blinking cowboys pointedly: "Who did you say is the boss of this outfit?"

"I was—er thought I was an hour ago," Gun Smith grinned as he stepped forward and grabbed Pecos Bill's hand. "But no more. Pecos, you beat us lone-handed and you beat us fair. An' when you beat a cowboy at his own little game, he's not the sort of critter to complain. I was the boss, but ain't no more. Pecos Bill, you're the boss this minute, and as far as I'm concerned, you're going to continue to be boss. I'm ready to eat out of your hand like a ding-busted cow pony!"

"Ye're right, Gun Smith, right you are," shouted a dozen hoarse voices. "Pecos Bill's an honest to goodness cowman an' no doubt about it."

"In that event," laughed Pecos Bill in high good humor, "since I'm to be the leader of your pack, or your boss, as you prefer to say, we'll ask Bean Hole to serve *Cow* for breakfast, the rawer the better!"

PART II

MODERN COWPUNCHING IS INVENTED AND DEVELOPED

V.

PECOS BILL INVENTS MODERN COWPUNCHING

All the men of the I. X. L. were eating out of Pecos Bill's hand within less than a week after he arrived. He took to the life of a cowboy like a duck to water. He learned their best tricks, then went on to do better. Gun Smith and Chuck and the rest were very soon like children before him. Among themselves, they bragged about their noble deeds; but when Pecos was around, they couldn't help thinking that they were mere bridled cayuses.

He could stand on the ground beside a broncho, turn an air flop, and land astride the pony before it had time to tighten a muscle. He could ride bareback without a bridle. He could urge his pony at top speed over ground so rough and uneven that Gun Smith and the others were afraid even to attempt it with bit and saddle. And he was so casual and modest about everything he did that they thought Pecos the eighth wonder of the world. Almost at once he was full of ideas. And what ideas!

Up to Pecos Bill's day, when a man wanted to capture a horse or a steer, he would lay a piece of rope down on the ground, make a loop in one end of it, sit down behind a tree or a blind, and by laying a bait, try to coax the wild critter to step within the loop. He would then jerk sharply on the rope, and perhaps one time in a dozen, if he was lucky, he would succeed in making a catch. It was no uncommon thing for a man to wait around and lose an entire month's time without laying hold of a single animal.

"Well, this sort of thing has got to be changed," said Pecos Bill to himself when no one was near to hear him. "A man can't be expected to waste his entire lifetime catching a single horse or cow."

Without further delay, Pecos got hold of the longest piece of rope he could find around the ranch, and began to throw it through the air. Next he rode off alone where the others could not see what he was doing. After three days of constant practice, he found that he could lasso almost anything. He was limited only by the reach of his line.

Pecos Bill would just make a large loop in one end of his rope, swing it wildly about his head three or four times, and then, with a quick flip of his forearm and wrist, send it flying like a bullet. And as he grew more and more skilled, he added rapidly to the length of his rope.

As soon as he was entirely sure of himself, Pecos asked the boys to come out and let him show them his new invention.

"See that roan steer across there? That's Old Crook-horn, our wildest critter, ain't it?" Pecos asked quietly.

Before anyone was aware of what he was doing, Pecos had whirled his loop about his head and had sent it so fast in the direction of the four-year-old, that the eye could scarcely follow it.

In an instant the old steer began to jump and bellow, and Pecos Bill to tow in the rope. Soon the astonished steer stood with lowered head before the even more surprised cowboys.

Not content with this great skill, Pecos began practicing from horseback.

In another week, he again called his cowboys out to see what he could do. They watched, with popping eyes, as he gave his rope a double turn around his saddle-bow. He then started his broncho at a hard gallop. They saw him quickly approach a rather tall, scraggly mesquite tree, whirl his loop wildly about his head and then fling it into the air. When he dragged a great hawk down from the topmost branch with the noose about its neck, the men were unable to believe their eyes.

"What sort o' wonder worker is this anyway?" they asked each other. "No human could ever throw the rope like that!"

Then Pecos Bill showed the men how it was done, and after two or three months of hard practice, each of them was able to make frequent catches at a distance of from ten to not more than twenty feet.

In the meantime, Pecos Bill had become dissatisfied with the fact that he couldn't find a longer rope. So he began to

The old way of roping an animal

braid himself a cowhide lariat. This is how he went to work. First he looked up some old horned steers that had lived so many years within the depths of the trees that there were green algae on their backs—moss-backs, sure enough. What's more, these steers were so old their faces were gray and wrinkled.

Whenever Pecos Bill got hold of one of these old fellows, he first loosened the hide behind the ears. He then grasped the steer by the tail and with a flip of his wrist and forearm and a wild yowl, he frightened the animal so that it jumped out of its skin. The tough hides of these old moss-backs were just what Pecos needed.

Three or four years later when he had it finished, his loyal ranchers declared on all sides that the lariat was as long as the equator, and that Pecos could lasso anything this side of China.

It was thus that Pecos Bill solved one of the problems that had worried cowhands and their bosses for years.

Another thing that Pecos very soon learned was that every ranch outfit was a bitter enemy of every other outfit. When two neighboring ranchers happened to meet anywhere near the supposed boundary of their pastures lands, they would begin to complain about missing cattle. Soon one would accuse the other of rustling—a polite word for stealing—his stock. Then there would be a sudden flashing of pistols, and one or the other, and often both men would bite the dust.

"Why do they all make such fools of themselves?" Pecos Bill asked. "Why don't they invent some way of marking their horses and cattle so that they will know them wherever they happen to meet them? All this fighting and killing is sheer nonsense. The spirit of the Coyote pack is entirely lacking."

While Pecos Bill was trying to invent a plan for marking the animals, a deer fly gave him just the right suggestion when it nipped him sharply on the arm. In chasing the fly away, he just naturally happened to notice the tattooed star that was his own mark of identification. "Mother was wiser than all these cowmen put together," Pecos declared, laughing at himself for having been so slow in finding the right idea! "Why of course cattle and horses can be tattooed the same way. Then they'll be marked for life."

That very evening Pecos Bill explained his plans to Bean Hole. The cook listened, then shook his head. "But tattooin' is too infernal slow," declared Bean Hole, looking at the purple markings up and down the backs of his own arms. "It wasted more'n a whole week of my time to do these pictures. It'd be quicker to burn the mark on. I ain't been cookin' all these years for nothin'. I know that if you burn the skin deep enough, it'll leave an everlastin' scar. Look at this mark now—I've been carryin' it on my wrist for more'n twenty-seven years, and it's just as plain now as ever it was."

"You're right," shouted Pecos. "Together we've invented a new system of bookkeeping for every cowhand in the world."

That evening Pecos explained the new invention to the cowboys, who were open-mouthed at the cleverness of the plan. Rusty Peters, who was a blacksmith by trade, was set immediately to make the brands. He bent the iron so that it would read I X L when burnt upon the side of a horse or a cow.

The next morning all the men were as excited as boys. They herded and roped the cattle, dragging them near the heated irons and throwing them on their side to apply the stinging brand. All day long the smoke curled. All day long the cattle bellowed.

"Keep that iron a cherry red, I'm a-tellin' you," shouted Bean Hole, as he gave directions. "Hold it on long enough to do more'n singe the hair. Wait till it smells like the Devil's own stithy, and looks like the whole critter was burned to a cracklin'. That's not near long enough. She'll shed that mark before the snow flies. There, that's about right. Let her bawl her fill. The loss of a few mouthfuls of hot air ain't going to hurt her any."

"Keep quiet, you old bag o' wind," shouted Rusty Peters, hard at work. "I ain't a blacksmith for nothin'! I'll burn a brand across your mouth in a minute if you don't keep quiet."

By evening the entire job was completed. It was found that the I. X. L. outfit possessed fifty-seven steers of various ages, forty-one cows, some fat and sleek, some spindly and thin, and twenty-four calves.

"This small herd ain't really enough to bother with," Pecos Bill observed in disappointment. "I thought you cowmen said you had a real ranch. Why, the woods are full of wild cattle that belong to nobody in particular. I'll just go out and drive in a few thousand of them. We'll put our trademark on them, and then they'll be ours."

"But how in tarnation will we ever keep these longhorns from runnin' straight away again?" asked Gun Smith with doubting stare. "What's the use of goin' through all this trouble disfigurin' the sides of all these cattle with our silly I. X. L. advertisement, if we're goin' to turn 'em back to the wild prairies again?"

Pecos Bill had not thought of this. The general custom among the cowmen had been to allow all the cattle to go and come whenever they liked. The ranch shack was nearly always built beside running water, and naturally, a few of the timid and lazy cows and steers would make this their home. The more ambitious stock would just as naturally wander off across the prairies and mesa and take refuge within the mesquite woods. Soon they would be as wild as deer and as difficult to catch.

This careless way of doing things meant that each ranch had a mere handful of shifting population, as far as the cattle were concerned. When the pasture and the water elsewhere were scarce, the cattle would flock to the ranch; but most of the time they would not even trouble themselves to take a French leave.

"It's dead wrong," said Pecos Bill to himself as he squatted on his haunches. "The problem to be solved is this: How are the cattle to be kept together in a herd after they are branded?"

While he was trying to work out the answer, he loped off alone to the top of a small mountain one morning before the others were awake. Far over the rolling prairies he could see many small wandering herds of cows and steers.

"Of course, if bad should come to worse, I could just round the herd up every night and throw my noose about them, and tie the cattle up till morning," he smiled. "But that ain't a good solution, for I can't bind myself that close to the ranch. I've got to reserve my energy for bigger work. All kinds of things are waiting to be invented."

At first as he sat and thought, his mind was just one grazing herd after another. He saw cattle scattered all over the prairies; he saw cattle stampeded, and he saw cattle leaving the herd to get lost in the wild mesa. But after a little things cleared up and he knew what he was going to do.

He got up, stretched the kinks out of his muscles and started at a brisk gallop for the ranch house. As soon as he arrived he called out for everybody to come.

"Here's the plan," he said excitedly. "The way to keep the herd together is for you men to ride out with the cattle every day. By waking up the drags and by holding back the leaders, the herd can be kept together and can be made to go to the best feeding grounds every day."

"You mean," said Gun Smith, with an ironical smile, "that us cowpunchers has got to be ordinary bovine critters the rest of our lives?"

"And stay with the herd all night and sleep with the hootowl?" asked Moon Hennessey sourly.

"Oh, yes," and the musical Mushmouth sang with a pretense of tears in his voice:

> "The centipede runs 'cross my head,
> The vinegaroon crawls in my bed,
> Tarantulas jump and scorpions play,
> The bronchs are grazin' far away,
> The rattlesnake sounds his noisy cry,
> And the Coyotes sing their lullaby,
> While I *sleep* soundly beneath the sky."

"It don't appeal to me," complained Moon Hennessey.

"Oh, well, you'll be just crazy about it when you've tried it —especially if the herd stampedes in your direction," suggested Gun Smith with irony. "It's goin' to be a regular picnic, Sundays and week days together, an' there's no doubt about it."

"And if the herd gets stampeded you'll be on hand to turn the leaders and start them milling until they are bitterly disappointed in trying to run away," added Pecos Bill quietly. "Besides, sleeping out under the stars is wonderful, once you've acquired the knack. I know from long experience."

"It'll all be easier than handlin' a month-old heifer calf," laughed Gun Smith bitterly.

"Well, now that we have decided what to do, I'll go out and drive in the cattle to be branded. And while I'm away Gun Smith will be your foreman. He'll keep you out of mischief. We can't get started too soon. So, with your permission, I'll be going right away. I'll have a herd ready to be branded first thing in the morning."

As soon as Pecos Bill had darted out into the night, the men began to wonder whether his coming to them had been a blessing or a curse.

"Chuck, before this monstrosity of yours arrived," began Moon Hennessey, "we was leadin' a peaceful and easy life. All we was expected to do was swap lies, and eat juicy tobacco. Now, it seems, we're goin' to be set at hard labor!"

"To my way of thinkin', the change will be all to the good," answered Chuck. "And who knows—it may bring us glory and honor—and gold!"

"Well, then, since I'm the appointed foreman of this outfit until Pecos returns," Gun Smith drawled as he put his hands on his guns, "I'm goin' to give you, Chuck, the place of highest honor. While the rest of us turn in for the night, you, Chuck, will take your Old Pepper and make contact with our branded herd. If they object to your presence and attempt to trample you and your noble steed to smithereens by startin' a wild stampede, you'll simply turn the leaders and set the herd millin'. If they show signs of thirst, you will lead them beside the still water!"

"Thank you very much for the honor," answered Chuck, as he rose promptly to carry out the assigned task.

"The rest of us motherless mavericks," Gun Smith continued, "will remain here, so's to be on hand with the ropes and the brandin' irons when Old Pecos returns any minute with his promised herd of wild cattle."

"Well," added Moon Hennessey with a bored yawn, "Old Pecos will be doin' splendid if he shows up by the end of next week. There'll be no herd here tomorrow mornin', I can promise you that."

"Don't fool yourself," replied Chuck spiritedly as he turned on his heel. "You evidently ain't yet acquainted with my brother."

"Brother!" fairly hissed Moon Hennessey in a rage. "Cut out your star identification talk and go on about your business!"

Next morning the men were awakened at early dawn by the dull thud, thud, thud of innumerable hoofs, and by the monotonous bawling of the weary cattle. As the men rubbed the sleep out of their eyes and looked about, they discovered, to their astonishment, that Pecos Bill had actually returned with a herd so large that they couldn't begin to see either its beginning or end.

"What, aren't you boys up yet?" Pecos called with a smile. "I've been having a wonderful night. And I've got enough cattle here to keep all of us busy for a while, anyway."

"Enough wild critters to keep the brandin' irons sizzlin' and the smoke risin' for a month of Sundays, I'd say," conceded Gun Smith, none too happily.

But Pecos Bill had no use for conversation just then. Breakfast was gulped down, cattle struggling and bellowing; the alkali dust flying mountain high; Bean Hole rushing about like a chicken with its head off, shouting his directions amid the din and waving his kettles and pans, and Rusty Peters keeping the smoking brands busy. This was the way it went all day long. By the time the sun had set, the tired men had added three hundred and thirty-eight cattle to their herd. Three hundred and thirty-eight—hurrah for Pecos Bill!

Pecos Bill himself was so happy over the results that frequently during the following months he would go out for an evening adventure, returning promptly the following morning with hundreds more bawling wild cattle. By the end of the season the I. X. L. ranch was one living sea of four-footed beasts.

As soon as his men had finished branding the incoming herd with the I. X. L. trademark, Pecos Bill at once began looking around to find other worlds to conquer. He instructed the men how to live in the saddle, and how to take cat naps astride their grazing ponies. He showed them how to soothe the cattle by crooning songs to them, and how to keep the herd together without annoying even the leaders.

When the herd stampeded, as it was sure to do at times, Pecos taught the men how to turn the leaders, and thus start the entire herd milling in a circle until the cattle finally winded themselves, and stopped through sheer weariness in the very spot from which they had started in the first place.

During these days, Bean Hole was the busiest man this side of Mars. After trying for a week to feed the men by carrying food out to them from the ranch shack, he finally gave up. On four or five different occasions, as he was starting out with his kettles and pans, he actually met himself on the trail coming back with the empty dishes of the previous afternoon. If he hadn't stopped his foolishness of trying to work twenty-seven hours a day just when he did, most likely his ghost would still be wandering on the wind over the same trails.

In the despair of complete exhaustion, Bean Hole finally hitched two spans of mules to the chuck wagon, loaded it down with enough food to last a fortnight, and left the ranch shack to take care of itself. He hadn't been gone half an hour before the place looked as deserted as the ruins of Pompeii.

Very soon the entire life of the ranch was going along according to the new plan. Everything was clicking like clock work and Pecos Bill was so pleased, for the present at least, that he couldn't think of anything left to invent. So he decided to go out and tell the world about what he had been doing, not for the sake of his own fame, but for the benefit of the cowmen of the entire range country.

One evening, after the cattle had settled down for the first sleep of the night, Pecos Bill announced to Gun Smith, his foreman, that it would be necessary for him to go away from the ranch for a few days. "If anybody asks where I am," he whispered, "just tell them that I'll be back for breakfast, like as not."

Pecos then took his boots under his arm, threw his coiled rope over his shoulder, and went bounding off across the rolling prairie. When he came to a strange ranch, he would quickly put on his boots and walk in great dignity, with jangling spurs, up to the boss of the outfit. Very soon he would be telling the wide-eyed cowman his story. In this way he easily covered forty or fifty miles in an hour and a half or two hours.

Pecos Bill thus visited all the ranches of the entire Southwest within two or three months. Not forgetting a single detail, he told the men everywhere what he had done. At first they thought him the biggest liar that had ever been invented in the whole world of cowmen. But when he had limbered up his lariat, and when they had witnessed his performance, they were quite willing to believe everything he told them.

What they saw was even more wonderful than what he had said. For with perfect ease, he would lasso any animal within reach of their vision. He could lasso a grazing or galloping steer, or lay his flying noose around the neck of a bald eagle in full flight.

The flying visits led later to many heated disputes among the puzzled ranchers: "You say this Pecos Bill left Hub's Ferry at nine o'clock? But he was at Slippery Mike's by eleven, and, that's a good forty miles as the crow flies, ain't it? And he was alone and on foot, wasn't he? Who is this Pecos Bill, anyway?" Every rancher seemed to have a bigger yarn to tell than his neighbor.

But they were all true—certainly! And through the efforts of Pecos Bill, ranchmen began to have a spring roundup and fall roundup. Pecos persuaded the ranchers of a given range section or river valley to drive together all the cattle of their entire district. They then sorted them into individual herds according to the particular brand of each owner. After this work was completed, each owner branded all of his calves. The strays, with no brand, and the orphan mavericks were then distributed equally and branded so that they could never again go astray. And every bit of the plan was Pecos Bill's.

In the fall the roundup was repeated so that the stray cattle could be located and given back to their rightful owners. After all the exchanges were made, the cowmen, as they took their herds back to their individual feeding grounds, found it easy to count the number of steers that were in condition for the market and the number that they would have to pasture during the coming winter.

Thus it was that each owner was given what belonged to him, according to the laws of reason, and not in accordance with the earlier outlawry of the pistol.

And so it came about very naturally, through the organization of all the scattered cowmen, that the fame of Pecos Bill rapidly spread to the four corners of the range country. From the valley of the Rio Grande, through Texas and New Mexico, Arizona and Colorado, Kansas and Nebraska, and far into the wilderness of Montana and Wyoming, cowboys, when they met, would carelessly throw one foot free from its stirrup and in a resting position shout to their nearest companion: "Say, have you heard about the rope Uncle Bill is still braidin' down on the Pecos? Why, it's already twice as long as the equator! You know, if Old Pecos Bill could only get a toe hold on the moon, he'd turn in and lasso this wanderin' planet of ours and bring it back into the Milky Way, where it belongs! Yes, and Pecos could do it easier than you or I could lasso a year-old heifer calf!"

VI.

PECOS TEACHES THE COWBOYS TO PLAY

As Pecos Bill thought over what he had already done, he saw that his work was not wasted. "The cowmen are beginning to learn to work together," he said to himself, "and that's very fine. What they now need most of all is to learn to play together. A little fun never hurts. Besides, the Coyotes long ago taught me that it's play that develops the spirit of the pack!"

And thus it came about that Pecos Bill began to invent

games for the cowpunchers. "I don't want them to be too easy," Pecos explained to Gun Smith. "And I want them to bring out everything the men have got in them. Let me see . . ."

It was at the beginning of the next fall roundup that Pecos Bill showed all the assembled cowmen and their cowhands what he meant. The fact is, he gave the first genuine exhibition of cowboy horsemanship and roping in the history of the world and the cattle country.

Sharing the secret with no one but Gun Smith, Pecos had for several months trained with various wild bronchos, especially roped for the purpose. When the time arrived for the play to begin, Gun Smith led a freshly roped wild broncho out into a wide stretch of mesa, skirted on all sides by the expectant cowpunchers, and then quickly removed the lasso. Pecos Bill, who was at the broncho's side, gave a sudden backward air flop and landed astride the startled pony. Pecos sat an instant on its shivering back and dug his clawed toes into its ribs, much as a monkey might have done.

The next instant Pecos let out the shrill blood call of the Mountain Lion and at the same time began to fan the broncho's ears with his ten-gallon hat. Needless to say, the pony began to buck furiously.

This was positively the first exhibition on this planet of real bucking. Before this time, no broncho had ever discovered in public that it was possible for it to cut up such outlandish capers. This particular broncho made the discovery through being scared almost out of its wits by Pecos Bill's unearthly yowl. When it began to buck, it went through all the antics of *sky scraping, cake walking, straight bucking, cork screwing, circling, pivoting, sunfishing, high sailing,* and *high diving.*

Everything that a broncho does to this day, that broncho did.

"The Devil's sure got into that calico horse," Old Baldy, a prosperous rancher, shouted as he jumped to his feet and waved his arms.

"Go to it, you calico horse! Wouldn't I like to be in that rocking chair! Say, I'd give my wages for the next ten years for the chance to ride like that!" Each and every man was shouting at the top of his lungs, so that he could scarcely hear what the next man to him was saying.

To cap the climax, the broncho very unexpectedly *sailed high,* and Pecos Bill flew from his back like a toy soldier and landed at what seemed almost a mile away. But he came down running, grabbed up his lariat and galloped back beside the defiant pony. With another perfectly timed air flop, Pecos Bill once more mounted his steed.

Again the broncho began *cake walking* and *high sailing,* but Pecos was more careful this time. He dug his clawed toes firmly into the animal's ribs and began coolly to do some fancy rope work with his lariat.

He started the large loop rotating into what to this day is called *spinning the wedding ring.* The wide loop slowly rose and fell over the head of the rider, then around the astonished broncho. The magical noose moved exactly as though it knew what it was going to do the next second.

When that broncho next started to *sail high,* the noose revolved swiftly on its spinning axis and the confused horse jumped suddenly through it, like a circus dog through a hoop.

A second later, Pecos Bill leapt lightly down from the winded broncho and ran to fetch a bag full of small objects. When the animal saw him returning this second time, it kicked up its heels and snorted in anger. Pecos simply turned another airy flip-flop and landed astride, as pretty as a picture.

Gun Smith now rode his own broncho alongside of Pecos Bill. Pecos threw all sorts of things into the air: hen's eggs, quarter dollars, and small bits of glass. With unerring accuracy, Gun Smith shot the yolks out of the eggs and pierced the quarter dollars through the center. Finally, Gun Smith fired his gun and Pecos fired his with such accuracy that he split Gun Smith's bullet in full flight.

"Who-ee!" shouted Old Baldy from the side line. "Git along, little dogie, and see this World's Wonder, Pecos Bill. He's no Coyote!"

"You can sort of see the clawed toes of the Coyotes, though!" replied the excited Big Bull with dry humor.

"Well, whoever he is, he's makin' the rest of us look like yearling mavericks!" continued Old Baldy.

Without warning, Gun Smith now drove a wild four-year-old Texas roan steer into the enclosure. Pecos borrowed Chuck's Old Pepper and rode alongside the snorting critter. And then Pecos performed—for the very first time in history —*bulldogging*.

He leaped from the back of the galloping broncho and, while he was still flying through the air, grabbed the fleeing steer by the horns. By immediately forcing his weight on one horn, he overbalanced the astonished beast and threw it heavily on its side. Before the felled animal had time to collect its senses, Pecos quickly grabbed it by one horn and by the tail and held it helpless on its side.

"Well, upon my life, I never thought I'd live to see anythin' like that. He's crazy!" gasped Old Baldy.

"Well, I'll be—" was heard on all sides.

Pecos had no sooner finished with the steer than Gun Smith

drove in a fresh bellowing brindle, mottled with white over the red. Pecos again leapt lightly into the saddle, and this time lassoed the galloping steer. With a quick tightening of the rope, he threw the lumbering beast.

Then he pulled the broncho up sharply on its haunches, anchored the taut rope with two half turns across the saddle horn, and springing from his steed, leapt across to the struggling steer and tied its four feet together with rawhide. Everybody today knows what that was—*hog-tieing*. But this was positively the first time it was ever done.

"Go to it!" shouted Old Baldy as he clapped his hands vigorously, "Pecos Bill, you're the World's Wonder."

When Pecos and Gun Smith had finished their part of the entertainment, Rusty Rogers did a turn to show his strength. He asked Pretty Pete Rogers to rope and hog-tie the largest yearling maverick he could find. Rusty took this calf first in one hand and then in the other, and lifted it arm-high above his head. The men applauded wildly and Old Baldy shouted:

"I'll be fleabitten, if it don't weigh a thousand pound, it don't weigh a thing!"

"Looks like we got another Hercules in our cow-camp," roared Big Bull.

Next Fat Adams gave the cowmen a sample of his ability to run away from his own shadow. He stepped forward to Old Baldy, held out his hand and said, "How do ye do?"

While Old Baldy was lifting his hand in greeting, Fat turned sidewise and vanished into thin air. When Old Baldy saw him next, he was standing ten feet away with his hand still extended.

"You must be seein' double," shouted Fat Adams. "I'm here, and not where you're reachin' out your paw."

"Old Baldy's been nibblin' too much moonshine again. He's seein' double," shouted the crowd, as they gave him the horse laugh.

"I'll be fleabitten . . . !" coughed Old Baldy.

The men had heard so much about Bean Hole's gyrating pancakes that they now called for him to show them his little trick. Bean Hole laid the batter in his frying pan for three cakes. When they were just right, he flipped the pan, and the cakes flew ten feet in the air, turned over, and returned to their places as pretty as you please. This the men thought very good.

Bean Hole flipped his next three cakes thirty feet into the air. When they returned to his frying pan this time, there were but two cakes instead of three.

"The big bad wolf has ate Little Red Riding Hood," Bean Hole informed them.

The men were now sure that Bean Hole was a magician, second only to Pecos Bill.

The third time, Bean Hole poured his batter into the middle of his pan and made one giant cake. He gave the pan a quick flip, and the cake flew fifty feet into the air before it turned over. He caught it in the very center of his frying pan without blinking an eyelash. When the cake was baked to a crisp brown on both sides, Bean Hole gave the frying pan an enormous flip.

The men saw the great pancake fly into the air like a whirling dervish. They watched it fly fifty feet, a hundred feet, a thousand feet, until it finally disappeared in the heavens. While they were still holding their breath in wonderment, Bean Hole quietly remarked:

"That one I'm donatin' to the Man in the Moon."

"Bless my bunions," Old Baldy cackled. "That pancake'll go right on gyratin' like one of the planets until we have a regular downpour of molasses rain."

The men cheered and cheered. Bean Hole's fame was secure.

"The show will not be complete," called Pecos, "without music. Mushmouth, show the boys what you can do on the lip-piano. And you, Bullfrog Doyle, come in with your foot-play. Strike up the dance!"

Mushmouth was so happy that he pressed a different mouth organ against either side of his jaw and played two tunes at the same time. And Bullfrog Doyle, not to be beaten, danced each of Mushmouth's tunes with a different foot. The men cheered and shouted and called them back again and again.

When Pecos Bill's program was at an end, the crowd pushed around him in excited delight. "Nobody but you could've thought it up," they declared.

But Pecos was modest. "We have joined to give you this little entertainment," Pecos smiled, "simply to introduce a little fun into our annual roundup. Every roundup should have a show—a Wild West show."

"You're right as usual," came the reply from a hundred different throats.

"This will be a good plan to follow," continued Pecos. "After each fall roundup we can give a first, a second, and a third prize for the best horsemanship. We can also give the same number of prizes for the best fancy rope work and the most skillful gun play, for the cleanest *bulldogging,* and also for the quickest job of *hog-tieing.*

"These various contests will furnish us a great deal of fun. Very soon it will come to be considered a high mark of honor to win any one of these prizes. To hear yourself declared the

Bean Hole and his gyrating pancakes

best man of the Range Country in one of these events will be a mark of distinction worthy of the hardest work."

"You're right again, as usual! But why did you wait so doggone long to show us what we should have known all along? Nine rousin' cheers for Pecos Bill!" came the hearty chorus from all the men.

Pecos could not help knowing that his actions and words had struck the hearts of his followers. The men had become boys again. Their blood was up.

Within a month the price of rawhide had doubled, and orders for cartridges had to wait several weeks before they could be filled. Moreover, every wild broncho on the range suddenly caught the bucking fever and in no time at all an order for a million saddle girths of extra width and strength was sent to New York. When the supply in America was exhausted, an extra order of another million was cabled to London. Before time for the next fall roundup cowmen everywhere on the plains were using two girths to each saddle instead of one. Yes, and new factories for lip-pianos and fancy cowhide boots and saddles were being built all the way from the Mississippi to the Atlantic.

Pecos Bill had awakened the spirit of play which had lain dormant on the range and this now came to life in good earnest. All across the wide prairie the cowpunchers were playing and singing and dancing and making preparations for carrying away one or more of the annual prizes.

Thus was started the regular yearly competitions that will continue as long as there are wild, bucking bronchos to be conquered, and as long as there are long-horned Texas steers to be laid low. And each succeeding year goes on adding its names to the lengthening rolls of honor.

Well, after all that had transpired, Pecos Bill couldn't be blamed for going back to the I. X. L. ranch from this particular roundup with a song in his heart. He had come up to the ranch house with his brother Chuck on that first notable day, expecting to find all *inhumans* poor creatures at best. Now he knew that the best there is in man is the very best there is anywhere. Not even his beloved Coyotes could equal this. Where muscle and nerve and honor and courage are caught in the saddle, there also rides manly joy.

VII.

PECOS BILL INVENTS THE PERPETUAL
MOTION RANCH

There was just one kink Pecos Bill never could get out of his rope. On his home ranch he was silently opposed by Moon Hennessey, who went about scattering poison among the minds of the cowmen.

"Before this here self-appointed dictator come to the I. X. L. ranch," Moon would say, "each of us was his own boss. We knew what real honest-to-God freedom was. Now we're forever dragged about in the noose and kicked about by the spurs of this upstart son of a Coyote! There is never a minute's time to rest. Huh! we're slaves, that's what we are, cowardly slaves!"

When the noise of this barking first came to the ears of Pecos Bill, he said nothing, but he did do a lot of thinking.

"I've simply got to invent a ranch that will run itself. A ranch where every job will be a snap—so easy that even Moon Hennessey will say that it's a child's play!"

The solution didn't occur to him at once. Pecos Bill's invention of a ranch that would run itself by perpetual motion evolved slowly in his subconscious mind.

But it arrived at last and in this way. One day Tim Toothacre, the boss of the Palo Pinto outfit, happened to mention a freak mountain he knew about. It was, in fact, the Pinnacle Peak that Paul Bunyan and his much-advertised lumberjacks had logged a dozen years earlier.

"It's what you might call a perfect mountain," Tim began. "It's as round as a silver dollar at the base, and it rises ten or a dozen thousand feet above the clouds, to a point so sharp an eagle couldn't hardly keep his balance on it. Its sides—now that the timber has been taken off—is covered with the finest bunch grass anywhere around. And it's so round it has a sample of every kind of weather there is. At its foot, on the sunny side it's summer all the time. Higher up it is always spring, and still higher it's winter all the time.

"I've often thought it wouldn't be a bad idea to own Pinnacle Mountain, for then you could have whatever climate you wanted. If you wanted it hot you could build your place on the sunny side where the mountain and the plains come together. If you wanted it cold, why, all you would have to do would be to set yourself at the top."

"And where do you say this Pinnacle Mountain is to be found?" asked Pecos Bill as if he weren't the least bit curious.

"It's called about a hundred and fifty miles from here, a trifle to the west of north as the crow flies," Tim replied. "And I've heard tell there's a lot of strange animals and birds there, too. You see, the sides is so regular and round that all the wild critters has to go around in circles. After a while they either wear off their leg or legs, as the case may be, on the side next the mountain. They say the rabbits there has two long and two short legs. They always run around the mountain the way the hands of a clock move. And there's a bird, called the Dodo, that has a long leg and a short one, a long wing and a short one. Yes, and they lay square eggs to keep 'em from rollin' down into the valley before they can be hatched. You see, once anything gets started rollin' down the mountain, it never stops till it's a mile away on the prairie."

"This is all mighty interesting," Pecos Bill said calmly.

"Yes, and the prairie dogs has one forepaw shorter than the other, and their noses sets at an angle so that when they start diggin', their holes'll be perpendicular and there'll be no danger of their rollin' out of their beds while they're asleep. And there's a mountain goat that has its legs shortened on one side and the horn it carries next the mountain is overweighted so that when it starts runnin' at full speed it'll be drawn in a circle. Otherwise, it would get goin' so fast that it'd fly off at a tangent. And the ears of the jackrabbits there is balanced just right. It's some place, Pecos."

"I'll have to take a run down that way when I find time some day and look the place over," Pecos rejoined, scarcely able to conceal his excitement.

Unfortunately, for a long time after this conversation, Pecos

Bill was kept too busy to think of anything beside getting the ranchers of the Texas valleys to co-operate in work and in play. But when this was finished, he decided to visit Pinnacle Mountain. He tucked his boots under his arm, threw his rope over his shoulder, and was there in three hours and ten minutes.

Pecos found Pinnacle Mountain even more perfect than Tim had described it. To make sure there was no mistake, Pecos loped around the base of the mountain two or three times searching for some slight imperfection; but search as he might he was disappointed, for everywhere it was as round as a silver dollar with all the milling around the edge worn off.

This so pleased Pecos Bill that he tried to find some imperfection on the sides of the mountain. He started to wind his way round and round the mountain. Up and up he went, up and up. Everywhere there was bunch grass. Everywhere there was smooth pasture land. Up and up he went till he struck the snow line. Beyond that he could see, between the clouds, the pointed peak glistening in the sunlight like the fixings on Mushmouth's lip-piano.

"Well, this is the most wonderful mountain I've ever seen or even heard about," Pecos said to himself. "If I hadn't actually loped about all over it, I never would have believed that everything could be so perfect."

As he started down the mountain he began searching for the strange animals and birds. By coming down in circles opposite to the way the animals traveled, he was able to catch them with no trouble at all. All he would have to do would be to scare up a jackrabbit. By running up the side of the mountain a few rods, he would then simply wait ten or fifteen minutes until it made its first round and pick it up as it passed.

The Dodo Birds

The jackrabbit, he found, was exactly as Tim had said. Its
_vo inside legs were shorter than its two outside legs. The
ear it carried next the mountain was twenty times larger than
its other ear. And it was the same with the Dodo bird. He
actually found one of these birds sitting on a nest of square
eggs. A little further down he came upon a nest that was
just hatched. Sure enough, the young birds were all headed
in the proper direction with their short leg next the mountain.

But the funniest thing Pecos saw was a colony of crooked-
snouted prairie dogs. They looked so comical and Pecos
laughed so hard at them, at first he couldn't do any thinking.
But as he turned away to leave something snapped inside his
head. "Why didn't I think of it before!" he shouted to himself excitedly. "This is just the place to start my perpetual
motion ranch."

Pecos Bill lost no time galloping back to the I. X. L.
boys. With his boots under his arm, he split the wind like a
swallow. The men were at breakfast when he came rushing
in, shouting: "I've got good news for you, boys. Get ready
to move the herd at once. Our ranch here is entirely too hard
to work. I've found a new location that will suit us all much
better. As soon as we can get ourselves settled, the new ranch
will run itself. There'll be absolutely no saddle work during
the day. There'll be no sitting up and singing songs all night
to keep the herd from stampeding. There'll be no driving the
herd to fresh pastures and to distant watering places, and no
need of the spring and the fall roundup. There'll not even be
any need of branding the calves. In fact, there can never be
a stray or a maverick. Really, it's the one ideal location for a
ranch in the whole world."

"Say!" growled Moon Hennessey to his nearest pal. "W... der where the Old Man gets all this Garden of Eden stu... I wish he'd forget all his silly nonsense."

"You don't really mean it!" snorted Gun Smith to Pecos Bill. "It's so sweet, it's almost sickenin'."

"Of course, I mean it," answered Pecos seriously. "Gun Smith, you take the men out and get the herd rounded up and ready to start in forty-five minutes."

"It can't be done that soon," objected the foreman. "Better make it three hours. Some of the steers is on the range at quite some distance from here."

"Well, what I mean is that we start immediately. That is, do not waste a minute in getting the herd in motion."

"Yes, sir," now replied Gun Smith, respectfully.

"Set the herd moving in a direction about two points to the west of north. I'll be with you to show you the way," Pecos answered in a tone of voice that meant no fooling. "You men had best pack your saddle bags. We'll not be coming back this way again—at least not for a long time."

"Yes, sir! Yes, sir!" answered the men as they set things in motion.

"And you, Bean Hole, get everything packed into the chuck wagon and don't waste any time."

"I'll be ready quicker'n you can say Jack Robinson," Bean Hole answered as he began stacking his kettles and plates and his slabs of bacon and his bags of corn meal.

Very soon the herd was on the march. All day long the cattle lumbered slowly forward. All day the men urged them on. Bean Hole brought up the rear with his chuck wagon and mules.

When night came Pecos Bill, with one jerk of his wrist,

threw the loop of his lasso completely around the entire herd to prevent their being startled into a stampede. The cattle seemed actually to like this, for they slept like kittens. Gun Smith and his men were thus given the chance to get their sleep, while the cows got up in the morning fresh for the journey of the day. At the end of a week the herd reached the foot of Pinnacle Mountain. Other ranchers usually found it very hard to move their herds an average of ten miles a day, but on this trip Pecos and his men had averaged twenty-six miles.

As they came to the foot of the mountain, Pecos Bill began eagerly: "Well, this is the place, boys! You see, we can simply take over a part of Paul Bunyan's cooking shack for our headquarters. At first we may have to spend some time getting the cattle used to grazing on the sloping side of the mountain. But as soon as this is done, we can give our spare hours to building a corral fence around the base.

"After this little chore is finished, there'll be nothing whatever to do but to sit around from morning to night, trying to find out who can tell the biggest lie. And when we get tired of tall talk, we can, for the sake of a change, try sticking to the truth for a day or two. Thus between Ananias and George Washington, we'll surely find plenty of chance for food and nourishment."

"But who will take care of the cattle?" asked Moon Hennessey. As usual he was finding fault.

"Why worry, Moon?" Pecos laughed. "The cattle will take care of themselves. There's an endless supply of bunch grass and plenty of fresh springs of clear, cold water. Yes, and there is every possible kind of climate. If the cattle become too hot in the sun, they can walk around on the other side of the mountain and find rest in the shade. If they are too cold, they can easily seek a sunny pasture. If the weather is too warm at a low altitude near the base, they can climb higher. If they feel chilly, they can go down where it's mild. There will always be as many kinds of weather as the most nervous steer can wish. If the storm rages on the north slope, the cattle can find refuge on the south slope; and if the storms happen to strike from the south, why, of course, the cattle can be depended on to put the mountain between themselves and the raging wind."

"It's all very wonderful, indeed," said Gun Smith, suddenly catching Pecos Bill's spirit of looking on the bright side of things.

"It's what I call the cowman's Garden of Eden!" Pecos laughed.

"Right you are," Gun Smith answered. "Adam and Eve never had half the snap that will soon be ours. All we'll ever have to do is to keep our corral fence in repair. Once in every full moon, say, we'll take a little pleasure jaunt around the mountain to see if maybe one or two of the posts or poles threaten to loosen up."

Suddenly carried away by the joy of the occasion, Mushmouth broke into a wild, free song. He played the melody on one side of his mouth with his lip-piano and sang the words with the other side:

> "Oh, glory be to me," says he,
> "And Fame's unfadin' flowers!
> All meddlin' hands are far away:
> I ride my good top-hawse today
> And I'm top-rope of the Lazy J—
> Hi! kitty cat, you're ours!"

It was in high spirits indeed that the work at Pinnacle Mountain started. The men at once began calling themselves the Lazy J outfit.

Moon Hennessey alone could see evil days ahead: "If any of them clumsy critters ever loses their footin', there's nothin' in God's universe—not even this corral fence we're goin' to build—will ever stop them. They'll keep right on rollin' till they get to Kansas City or Chicago. And by the time they've stopped, there won't be enough left of 'em to make a decent hamburger steak!"

Soon Pecos Bill started to build the fence. He went out one morning before the men were awake and called at the settlement of straight-snouted prairie dogs beside the foot of the mountain. After giving a dozen squeaks and grunts in the prairie dog language, Pecos had the whole colony out of their houses, twisting their noses and paying strict attention to each word that he told them.

"Every place I leave the print of my boot heel there one of you must dig a hole, do you understand?"

Every prairie dog wriggled his friendly snout and squeaked: "Yes, we all understand."

"Very well, my little brothers," Pecos squeaked in reply. "Follow me."

The scampering colony was immediately at his heels. "Dig the holes deep and straight," Pecos squeaked as he ran along. "Here is the place to begin."

Pecos Bill started on the jump and at regular intervals of ten feet he left a deep print of his heel. One prairie dog stopped at each heel print and started immediately to dig his well. The others scampered on, ready to take their turn.

By the time Gun Smith and his men were ready for break-

fast, Pecos had covered the entire twelve or fifteen miles
around the foot of the mountain and was ready to eat. At
the end of the meal he announced quietly what he had done.

"Well, I've made a start. The post holes for our corral fence
are all dug."

"What kind of a joke do you call this, anyway?" asked
Moon Hennessey in a loud voice.

"You see, I simply asked the colony of prairie dogs to help
me," replied Pecos dryly. "Together we did the entire job in
just forty-eight minutes!"

After breakfast Pecos told Gun Smith to direct the men in
setting a post in every hole. This was not hard to do, for Paul
Bunyan had left plenty of unused scraps of cedar that were
the right size.

The next morning Pecos began loosening the hide behind
the ears of each of his old moss-horned steers. Then he
grabbed each by the tail and scared him so that he simply
jumped out of his skin. He cut these hides into leathern
thongs and taught the men how to lash the poles to the posts.
As soon as the thongs had shrunk in drying, the fence was as
solid as a stone wall.

Before Pecos Bill had finished there were a lot of forlorn-
looking naked old critters sneaking about, trying to hide
themselves until they grew other skins. Every one of these
steers had previously been skinned at least once, and some of
the older and tougher ones twice.

By wasting no time, Pecos and his men were able to complete the entire twelve miles of corral fence in four days and
a half.

"Well, we may as well call it a week, in round figures,"
laughed Pecos, very well satisfied with the spirit shown by

Pecos Bill demonstrates the method of making an animal jump out of its skin

Gun Smith and the others. "It would have taken an entire week, too, if it hadn't been for the fact that the prairie dogs did their bit in helping us out with the post holes."

"I wonder how long it'll be," asked Moon Hennessey in doubt, "before our steers begin to wear off their legs on the near side so's to be able to get around on the side of the mountain without limpin'."

"Time alone will tell," answered Gun Smith with curt brevity.

VIII.

PECOS BILL GENTLES THE DEVIL'S CAVALRY

Pecos Bill had taught the cowmen how to raise steers and had instilled the spirit of play into their work, and so the Valley of the Rio Grande was beginning to be crowded with herds of cattle. Even a state the size of Texas seemed entirely too small to pasture the rapidly multiplying live stock.

The American Indians of the Southwest, of course, entirely misunderstood what was happening. They had, for centuries, been accustomed to prey on the buffalo, and now they insisted on killing the cattle. The result was that the Government at Washington established Military Posts and placed the Indians on Reservations.

With the rapid increase in the number of cattle, the price of beef broke sharply. The Military Posts offered the best market, for after corralling the Indians, the Government was obliged to furnish them with meat.

There developed, naturally enough, a great many cattle rustlers, or, in plain language, thieves. These men had in the past followed the herds of buffalo and had shamelessly slaughtered them for their skins. They were called skinners, and now that the buffalo had become scarce, these skinners found it easy to become outlaws. They were used to getting something for nothing. Why not keep right on?

This is exactly what they did. They would swoop down upon a choice herd that was grazing far out on the range. Then they would fall vigorously upon the cowpunchers who were on guard, accusing them of stealing the cattle. The rustlers would, of course, claim that they themselves were the rightful owners of the herd, and with high-powered rifles across their saddles, they would quickly drive the cattle away to their own ranch.

Among the most notorious of these gangs of rustlers was the Devil's Cavalry. Their ranch was known far and wide as Hell's Gate Gulch, where Nature had, it seemed, formed a perfect refuge for them. For this ranch of theirs was a large box canyon with abrupt, rocky ledges and impenetrable chains of hills upon all sides. Between these hills lay a fertile spreading valley.

There was but a single entrance to the canyon and this lay through a long, tortuous, rippling stream of water that ran between precipitous rocks. It was thus easy for the Devil's Cavalry to lead astray all who tried to follow their trail. Only one cowboy had ever been clever enough to solve the mystery of the entrance, and upon entering the canyon he was immediately riddled with bullets. Only a short corral fence across the dancing stream was needed to secure the stolen cattle from all danger.

Whenever the gang brought a herd of cattle into their secluded box canyon, they quickly covered the original brand of the rightful owner with a larger brand of their own. This brand was in design a large wheel with spokes so thickly set that their impression easily covered any other brand of the entire Range Country.

They were such daring rascals that they were always on hand when the Government Military Posts needed a fresh supply of beef. And they had no difficulty selling their stock, for theirs was always the choicest herd of steers to be found anywhere.

Many frontier towns had, by this time, sprung up over night like mushrooms. They were made up of hastily constructed shacks, and served as trading posts and supply camps. Very soon their citizens discovered that the cowpuncher craved excitement. Bars were established. The Indian's fire water flowed freely. After long months of hard riding in the saddle, in the cowboys came to blow in half a year's wages in a single night.

Now the leaders of the Devil's Cavalry liked nothing better than galloping into Dallas, one of the most lively of the frontier towns. There they would gulp down a glass or two of whiskey, then stagger out into the street with the open intention of scaring the natives out of their skins.

Old Satan, one of their most feared leaders, would then swagger about, pretending to be drunk, brandishing pistols, and singing out in a thick voice: "I'm the toughest, wildest killer in the land of the Rio Grande. I'm so tough I eats raw hide without boilin' it. When I'm really hungry, I bites off the ears and snouts of grizzly bears. When I meets a rattlesnake, I gives him the handicap of takin' the first bite. I've killed a lot of them rattlers that way by givin' them a drop or two of my own hydrophobia. I lives in a box canyon where the air is so plumb full of lead bullets there ain't hardly any air left to breathe. The further up the canyon you goes, the wilder and woollier the inhabitants gets. I lives at the very top end! It's so hot up there that when one of our outfit dies and arrives in hell he naturally sends back for his blankets to keep him warm!"

Then he would sing this ditty:

"I'm wild and woolly and full of fleas,
I'm hard to curry beneath the knees,
I'm a he-wolf from Hell's Gate Creek,
I was dropped in thunder from a lightning streak,
And it's time to shoot up the town! Whoopee!"

After carrying on like this until he actually became bored at frightening innocent people he and his companions would end by shooting up the town. They would take anything that they wanted from the shelves of the various stores; then dare the shopkeepers, if they weren't satisfied, to ride out to Hell's Gate Gulch and settle the scores. They punctuated every statement by a bullet hole through a lamp globe or a window pane, with the result that when it was noised about that the Devil's Cavalry was entering town, the officers of the law would sneak away and hide until these fearsome desperadoes were at a safe distance on their way home.

Things got so bad finally that the Government offered a reward of $500 for the capture of the gang, dead or alive.

Just about the time this reward was posted, Pecos Bill had everything organized up on Pinnacle Mountain. So he thought he'd take a little time off himself. Leaving things in care of good old Gun Smith, he loped off to Dallas, his boots under his arms, and his lariat over his shoulder.

The Devil's Cavalry had just cleaned out the town the day before his arrival and everybody was as unstrung as a lassoed wild broncho. When Pecos Bill walked innocently into the general store, his chest was high and his spurs jingled merrily. The proprietor changed his cud of tobacco, twiddled at his rawhide suspenders, looked out of the corner of his eye and prayed that this might not be another visitor from Hell's Gate Gulch.

Pecos Bill merely smiled as he listened to the fearsome tales of the desperados, and said coolly when he had heard it all:

"Where did you say this Hell's Gate Gulch happens to be?"

"Well, nobody knows for sure," the man answered in a fidgety tone, "but everybody is about positive it's up the North Fork of the Red River, in the Wichita Mountains."

"And which is the shortest cut to take to get to the place?" Pecos Bill asked.

"Get there, did you say?" the storekeeper repeated in a tone that clearly indicated Pecos Bill could not possibly be in his right mind. "Why should you want to know?"

"Only because I'm going to make these cattlemen a visit. I think I'd like to meet them."

"You ain't an outlaw, too, be you?" asked the startled proprietor. "Or are you looking for the most painless way of gettin' off the earth for good?"

"You entirely misjudge me," replied Pecos Bill quietly. "I'm

The Devil's Cavalry

an ordinary cowpuncher, looking for a little Sabbath day quiet."

"Well, you're a strange cayuse," commented the storekeeper as he shifted his quid of tobacco.

Pecos continued to ask questions until he learned the quickest trail for going to the Gulch. Then he bought himself the best horse and saddle that he could find in Dallas, for he thought he would appear less suspicious if he rode rather than went on foot.

"The thing I don't like about this journey," he said to himself after he had ridden most of the day at breakneck speed, "is that it's so slow. If I'd only dared to pull off my boots and gallop across the mesa alone, I would have been knocking at Hell's Gate door hours ago."

It was at high noon on the second day of his journey, as Pecos Bill was urging his broncho forward at a sharp gallop, that he met with misfortune. By this time, he had reached the foothills of the Wichita Mountains, and his instinct told him that the Gulch was but a short distance ahead.

Then suddenly things began to happen. The Granddaddy of all the Rattlesnakes, as large around the middle as a man's thigh and at least a dozen feet long, sat up at the side of the trail, hissed viciously, and made an angry strike at the passing broncho's leg. The horse bounded quickly aside, stepped into a prairie-dog hole, and broke his left front leg just above the pastern. Pecos leapt to the ground, drew his pistol, and without delay, put the suffering animal out of its misery.

But the great Rattlesnake had, by this time, coiled itself directly in front of Pecos Bill. This was rather annoying, for with saddle and bridle in hand, Pecos was in a hurry to proceed on his journey.

"What do you want?" hissed Pecos, talking to the snake in its own language.

"You're the son of the Coyotes I heard about years ago, if I'm not mistaken. Now do you know me? I've waited for years to get back at you!" hissed the snake between lightning flashes of its tongue.

"You've already done it," hissed Pecos. "Get out of my way before I jerk off your head. I'm in a big hurry!"

The snake now moved even more directly in front of Pecos, darted its great flat shining head back and forth, and shot out its nervous forked tongue still farther as it spoke: "You can't fool me! I know who you are. I've had to listen to entirely too much talk about what a wonder you are. And I don't believe a word of it. The Coyotes coddled you so much you haven't any strength of your own. Now I'm going to show you what's what and who's who!"

"Is that so?" replied Pecos with a prolonged hiss, and his tongue fairly shot fire as he spoke. "Well, come on, show what's back of that bragging you've been doing all these years. I'll give you the first three bites. Get out of my way, or you'll be sorry!"

"Sorry! Pooh!" retorted the snake with biting sarcasm. "Go tell your story to a Porcupine! I've taken care of myself entirely too long to be frightened by any silly child of the Coyotes!"

Pecos threw down his saddle and bridle, and there followed a fight the like of which a snake and a man never waged before. The snake would fling its weight forward, then retreat, like lightning. Pecos would dodge its thrusts, instantly follow its recoil, then give it a quick jab with his spur. In no time at all the snake was so furious it began to strike blindly. Pecos, the while, prodded it more and more cruelly with his jagged heels.

"Had enough yet?" Pecos hissed with a hint of ironic laughter.

This but enraged the venomous monster all the more. Its great eyes glared in fury, and it continued to strike aimlessly here and there and everywhere in its blind rage.

Now Pecos knew the moment had come. Leaping forward, he caught the writhing serpent securely by the throat. Then Pecos merely smiled and pressed his powerful fingers more tightly about its throat and shook its head more and more violently, as it lashed furiously at him with its mighty tail.

"Well, well!" Pecos remarked casually. "Haven't you had enough yet?"

With that the Rattlesnake gave up. Its tail hung limp and to the best of its ability—which was none too good—it smiled ingratiatingly. "Have mercy, Pecos Bill," it fawned, "I, too, love my life. I am only a poor, proud, foolish creature. I should have known better than to attack you. I've heard a hundred times how wonderful you are. Now I believe every word of it. If you will but spare me, I'll be your willing slave as long as I live."

"Now you're talking sense," said Pecos Bill. "Lift up your head and look me square in the eye. That's right. Now do you promise me solemnly that you will do exactly as I tell you?"

The Rattlesnake promised without any exception to do exactly whatever Pecos asked.

"Very well," concluded Pecos Bill. "I will give you my word of honor that if you obey as you have promised, I will be your best friend. No harm shall come near you as long as you obey. But let me see one false move on your part, my friend, and I'll show you no mercy!"

"It is agreed," hissed the snake in humble submission.

"Very well, then, listen to these my words," answered Pecos Bill. "Wrap yourself twice about my left arm. Carry your head well forward and your tail well behind. You will thus prove an additional eye to me as I go forward."

The snake immediately wrapped itself about Pecos Bill's left arm near his shoulder. Then Pecos picked up his saddle and bridle again and galloped off on his own feet toward Hell's Gate Gulch.

After another hour Pecos arrived at the shallow dancing river and started leaping merrily along the narrow shore. As he was passing under an overhanging crag of granite cliff, the Rattlesnake suddenly hissed: "The Wouser! The Wouser leaps!"

Pecos Bill had just time to dodge as the fierce, growling animal, which looked like a cross between a Mountain Lion and a Grizzly Bear and which was almost twice the size of a broncho, landed not ten feet in front of him.

"Good afternoon, Mr. Wouser," growled Pecos Bill fiercely in this latest enemy's own language.

"Good afternoon," replied the Wouser sheepishly. "I'm sorry if I frightened you, but, you see, I just slipped off the overhanging cliff. I surely hope I haven't scared you too much!"

"You haven't frightened me at all, I assure you," answered Pecos Bill serenely, in the same breath hissing to the Rattlesnake to free itself from his arm. The snake obeyed instantly and sat down in a coil close beside the saddle and bridle to watch the fun.

"By the way," smiled the Wouser as though he had met

his very best friend, "I've heard a lot about you, Pecos Bill."

"Yes, and I've heard a lot about you," smiled Pecos in answer.

"Who's been talking about me again?" snapped the Wouser, suddenly revealing his bad temper.

"Oh, your neighbors—the Grizzly Bear and the Porcupine and the Skunk and the Coyotes and the Cowboys have all told me much about your pleasant ways!"

"Now you're only making fun of me," snarled the Wouser with a nasty roar. "Haven't the old hunters ever warned you that, once you allow yourself to get within my power, you'd better say your prayers?" And the Wouser licked his hungry chops in a superior manner.

"Yes, so I've heard often enough," replied Pecos Bill as he coolly buttoned his coat close about him. "But you must remember, Mr. Wouser, that I'm not exactly an old hunter, and what's more, I am not yet within your power!"

"Is that so?" snarled the Wouser. And without more ado he leapt viciously at Pecos Bill. But Pecos Bill was ready for him. He sprang past, and the fierce Wouser discovered to his amazed disgust that his claws were clutching nothing at all.

In his rage, the Wouser gave his terrifying shriek of blood. Pecos Bill, not to be outdone, mocked the Wouser in his own hideous language of blood, and the fight was on in earnest!

Even the Rattlesnake with his piercing eyes was unable to follow their fast and furious movements. Every time the Wouser leapt at Pecos Bill he would find, the next second, that he had missed his catch. And each time that the Wouser flew past him, Pecos would tear out a large handful of his fur and fling it into the Wouser's eyes.

No wonder the Wouser completely lost his head and roared

and leapt wildly in every direction. Pecos kept a cool head. He snatched away great bunches of his fur and threw them into the infuriated animal's face. The Wouser, in his fury, raised his muzzle and shrieked, and the fur was blown straight up into the sky. After two or three hours of this, the sky was so filled with the Wouser's fur that darkness began to fall and the Devil's Cavalry, who were up on top of Hell's Gate Gulch, thought there was an eclipse of the sun.

Finally the Wouser couldn't keep it up another minute. Brushing the fur out of his bloodshot eyes, he sat back on his quivering haunches. As soon as he had gotten back his breath, he said politely:

"What are you so excited about, Pecos? Can't you take a little joke?"

"I'm not excited in the least," replied Pecos Bill blandly. "Really, you know, I haven't enjoyed myself so much in a month of Sundays." The fact was that Pecos Bill was completely stripped to the waist and his pantaloons were hanging in shreds and his back and sides were gashed with long red marks from the cruel claws. But Pecos Bill didn't mind.

"Very well, then," barked the Wouser with affected courtesy, "I'll just bid you good day and wish you much happiness during the remainder of your journey."

"You'll do nothing of the kind!" roared Pecos Bill, slapping the Wouser sharply across the muzzle. And to point up his words he stepped back and put his hand on the butt of his pistol.

"You should have known better than to tackle Pecos Bill, my brother," hissed the Rattlesnake.

"You have bragged long and loud, Mr. Wouser," declared Pecos, "of the day and the hour when you would meet me.

Now you are going to listen to what I have to say. I'm on my way to pay a visit to the Devil's Cavalry up at Hell's Gate Gulch. Step over here lively while I bridle and saddle you. If you make a single false move, a bullet from this gun will set you right."

"Just as you say," barked the Wouser, quite crestfallen, "not that I care in the least."

Within the next minute, Pecos Bill was aboard the great leaping Wouser and was quirting him unmercifully across the ribs and rump with the Granddaddy of all the Rattlesnakes. They were soon splashing at such a lively lope up the rippling ladder of river that they never even saw the corral fence at the mouth of Hell's Gate Gulch until they were right upon it. But it didn't worry them in the least. They cleared it by ten feet.

While all this was happening the fur in the sky was gradually settling down and the light of the sun was beginning to come back. The Devil's Cavalry were squatting on their heels, lazily whittling with their great bowie knives and bragging about what terrible villains they were. How they did laugh at the creamy-faced loons down at Dallas! "Why, you could tip any man there over with a feather duster any day you happen to be down town!"

Old Satan was talking the loudest and the biggest of the whole crowd. He was bragging about eating rawhide without boiling it, and about giving a Rattlesnake the handicap of the first bite. He was just saying how he'd been raised on prickly pears and had learned as a boy to whip alligators and grizzly bears. He was just in the middle of this rollicking little ditty:

> "I'm wild and woolly and full of fleas,
> I'm hard to curry below the knees—"

when Pecos Bill drew in rein; and the gaunt Wouser's great claws dug streams of fire from the flinty rock as he came to a slithering stop on his haunches directly in front of the assembled members of the Devil's Cavalry.

Pecos Bill climbed with cool unconcern from his Wouser and, gun in hand, hung the great limp Rattlesnake deliberately across his saddle horn. Then he brought his jingling spurs noisily together and calmly and fearlessly stood before the members of the Devil's Cavalry.

This unprecedented performance so amazed the men that they only stood and stared.

Without a sign of fear or concern, Pecos Bill very firmly said:

"I'm here to interview the Boss of the Devil's Cavalry!"

There was an awed silence for a full minute. The men were all so startled out of their wits that for at least five minutes they looked like frozen statues. Then two or three got so nervous that they tumbled over backwards off their heels and lay like logs on the ground. After a long, awkward pause, Old Satan, a giant five feet and nineteen inches tall, bedecked with six pistols and ten bowie knives, got up stiffly on his hind legs. He twisted the ends of his elegant mustache and with teeth chattering managed to remark: "The only piece of human flesh alive that's big enough or got backbone enough to boss the Devil's Cavalry is you, Pecos Bill! You don't need to think that I don't know all about you! You're the only man in the world I've ever admitted was better than I am. Here, take my gun and take my pet bowie knife. They're yours from now on. You're the Boss, the new Boss of Hell's Gate Gulch!"

While Old Satan was making his speech the other members

of the Cavalry were regaining poise sufficiently to whisper among themselves: "This Pecos Bill must be some rider! Just think of the amount of sagebrush and cactus needles it must o' took to scratch the sides off him and his Wouser like that!"

PART III

PECOS BILL ROAMS THE SOUTHWEST

IX.

PECOS BILL BUSTS PEGASUS

Pecos Bill very soon found that Old Satan, Gabriel and the
rest were at best only tall talkers. Their chief occupations
were whittling and seeing who could tell the biggest yarn.
They'd just had luck in finding Hell's Gate Gulch, that's all.
And what with never having to do much serious work and
doing tall talking most of the day, they'd come actually to
believe their whoppers. Oh, without a doubt they were the
most fearsome outfit in existence, so terrible that the Devil

136

himself would put up his hands in horror when they arrived in force at the gate of hell.

They did, however, have the most wonderful herd of bronchos that Pecos Bill had ever laid eyes on. Success in rustling cattle depended so much on good horses that these men simply had to have them or else quit their outlaw business.

Quite honestly Pecos Bill praised them for their wonderful cowponies.

"Oh, we got the best horses in the Range Country," Old Satan bragged, as he twisted his long mustache. "Wherever we find a piece of horse flesh we take a fancy to, it's the same as ours. Whoever has it either gives it to us, or else we takes it, as the case may be, and that ends that."

"How interesting," Pecos remarked politely.

"There's just one horse in this world we've wanted that we never could lay hands on," Old Satan continued. "We've heard about him for years. All the way from Canada to Mexico he's known as the Pacing White Stallion. Two years ago the twenty-first day of last May, we was ridin' up Powder River basin, thinkin' of nothin' in particular, when the event occurred. We suddenly spied the White Stallion, the most glorious Palimino under high heaven, with a herd of the grandest mares you can imagine.

"I tell you, that stallion's head and tail was right up in heaven, and he snorted sparks of fire out of his nostrils. And it's the truth that there was a greenish-red light that said as plain as the nose on your face: 'You fellows think you're some riders. Well, if you still think so, come on and see!'

"Now, the Devil's Cavalry ain't the men to swallow a dare like that, you can bet. So we sets out to capture Mr. Pacing White Stallion. The stallion's shrill bugle sets his mares flyin' at his heels. We quirted our own horses for several miles over the soap weed mesa, but his slowest mare outdistanced us like we was babies. And Old Pegasus, for that's what we named him then and there, never went beyond a sort of daredevil pace. It was the most provokin' experience!

"Well, when our horses was completely winded, we stopped to rest 'em. We swore before we started home that we'd tame that stallion, if it was the last thing any of us ever did do.

"As we rode back to Hell's Gate Gulch we tried to figure out how to get our hands on him. And after we'd refreshed ourselves and our cayuses for a week we sets out again. Each of us took a string of six of our best horses—which is the same as sayin' the best horses in the Southwest Range Country, as well you know. We studied the lay of the land for a few days till we'd discovered where every trail led.

"Then each of us took his station at a different place—each at some strategic point, as you might say. What we was goin' to do was to walk him down. That is to say, each of us was goin' to ride at his heels for a few hours, then to pass him on to the next fellow who was waitin'. We'd keep it up, day after day, until Mr. Pegasus would just naturally have to give in. Oh, it was a good plan, if I do say so.

"Well, when the day for startin' the race came, that stallion snorted out his bugle nearest to where I was waitin'. So I took up the trail first. I rode at top speed for two or three hours, changin' horses every fifteen minutes. And I went so fast you couldn't see me pass.

"After three hours, I passed Mr. Pegasus on to Kingdom Come, here. Kingdom was waitin' with as fine a string of horses as ever felt neat's leather. He went as fast as I did, then passed the stallion on to Gabriel.

"Well, we kept that race goin' from daylight to dark, day in and day out for a full week. After two or three days our mares had all fallen out by the wayside. But we let 'em lay, givin' 'em no more attention than as if they'd been crippled jackrabbits.

"Once or twice every day, one or the other of us would hear that stallion neigh and now and then we'd catch a glimpse of him, as fresh as an April mornin'.

"Well, at the end of a week we was a sorry outfit and no mistake. The gopher holes and the rocks on those slopes had just about done us up. We had to shoot a dozen of our choicest buckaroos because of broken legs. And most of the others wasn't worth takin' home, they was so broken-winded and lame. All told, we looked about like a lead dollar. And what we said on the way back here I'm not tellin' you.

"That Pegasus had called our bluff completely. And when we'd gotten back our breath so's we could argue out every point pro and con, this is what we decided. This stallion wasn't no ordinary horse, because, well, it didn't stand to reason that any horse with human broncho blood in his veins could behave in any such fashion as this fellow had done. Any broncho in this here range country would've completely broken inside of three days at most. And no horse livin' could have kept on as easy as he had when all the other horses was strainin' every muscle on the run.

"This fellow, we decided, must have been sired by that flyin' horse you hear so much talk about in story books. I mean the first Pegasus. And I wouldn't be surprised if he has wings, too. I tell you we'd spurred and quirted like nobody's business, and our horses galloped like mad, but that stallion, he never broke down his consarned pace."

Pecos Bill listened more and more intently until Old Satan had finished his story. When Old Satan explained how the stallion's father must have been the real Pegasus, Pecos could scarcely sit still.

"Just how far is it to this Powder River?" Pecos asked.

"Well, it's just about an even hundred miles," Old Satan replied slowly as he calculated the distance.

"With your permission, I'll turn the management of this Hell's Gate Gulch back into your hands at once. Then I'll be on my way. I'm looking for a little excitement, don't you see?" Pecos Bill explained with seeming unconcern. "I'll just take my saddle and bridle and go out and see if I can't capture this magic-winged horse."

Old Satan strongly urged Pecos Bill to take the favorite cow-pony of the Gulch, Bald Eagle. Pecos, however, replied softly:

"I have nothing against your broncho, you understand, but when I'm in a hurry I always prefer to go on foot."

Old Satan was at first visibly offended. But when Pecos Bill tucked his boots quickly under his arm, threw his saddle and bridle and lariat across his shoulder, and loped off at such incredible speed as the Devil's Cavalrymen had never seen, Old Satan was somewhat reconciled.

"What kind of critter is this Pecos Bill, anyway? He made the Wouser eat out of his hand, as you might say. Now he's runnin' faster'n a speedy bronch!" they all exclaimed as he vanished from their sight.

As soon as Pecos Bill arrived at Powder River he gave the shrill bugle of a stallion, and the next minute there came back on the wind a neigh so defiant that Pecos Bill trembled. But that didn't keep him from letting out another bugle as defiant as the first.

When, a few minutes later, the beautiful white stallion came prancing around a clump of sage brush, he was alone, just too proud to be seen with ordinary horses. Pecos Bill held his breath. This magnificent horse, with feet that seemed scarcely to touch the ground, with head and tail right in heaven just as Old Satan had said, completely fascinated him.

Pecos Bill maintained the pose of invisibility that the Coyotes had taught him until the stallion got to within a few paces of him. Then he stood up and talked in horse language.

But that stallion couldn't be fooled. He just stamped his front feet, snorted in disgust at seeing a mere *human,* and then whirled on his heels in the direction of his feeding grounds.

As quick as greased lightning Pecos Bill flung his lariat, and the sliding noose fell with perfect accuracy over the stallion's neck. When Pecos tightened the lariat, the stallion wheeled facing him, reared high on his hind legs, brought his forefeet down right where he wanted to, and broke the taut buckskin as if it were nothing but a whipcord. Then he shook the noose from his neck, whirled on his heels again, and pranced away as lightly as if on the wings of the wind.

Watching him go, Pecos Bill felt—for the first time in his life—the lust of greed. Never before had he cared to call anything his own; but now he wanted nothing in the world so much as this glossy white Pegasus.

Quickly flinging aside his lariat, his boots and his saddle, Pecos Bill fairly flew in pursuit of the retreating stallion. At first, the stallion snorted derisively in horse language which Pecos clearly understood: "You're the first human who has ever been foolish enough to try to catch me lone-handed. What have you been doing, feeding on the loco weed? You're not quite in your right mind—that's my opinion."

Pecos Bill didn't stop for mere words. He just quickened
his pace until Pegasus was forced to break into a stiff gallop.
It was the first time in his life that Pegasus had been forced
to go faster than a pace, and so, very soon, he began to have
the greatest respect for Pecos Bill.

This was merely the beginning of what soon proved to be
the greatest of all recorded races. For three days and four
nights the flying hoofs were chased closely by the flying feet.
From Mexico to Canada and from Canada to Mexico the
pair kept up their fast clip. The two contestants were so even-
ly matched that neither could gain on the other. Down into
cavernous gullies, beside mirroring lakes and through raging
torrents, up the steepest of cliffs and across sage and soapweed
and cactus, over fertile valleys and sweeping rolling mesa,
along mountain sides where the view was superb, and through
blinding, stinging mesquite, the stallion went madly on, hop-
ing against hope to shake off his desperate pursuer. And
wherever Pegasus led, Pecos Bill followed.

By the time the race was finished they had galloped three
times around the state of Texas; they had made a bee line
across the Llano Estacado or Staked Plain; they had eaten
the alkali dust of New Mexico; they had touched the high
spots of Colorado; they had skirted the plains of Kansas and
Nebraska; they had crossed into Canada and had leapt the
chocolate waters of the Missouri; they had taken the Arkansas
River at a bound; and had finally returned to their starting
point, the valley of the Powder River.

At length, on the morning of the fourth day, Pecos Bill
thought of a bit of strategy. The stallion, at the time, was
running down a trail that was bordered on its left by a long
overhanging shelf of limestone. By leaping upon this, Pecos

Pecos Bill busts Pegasus

reasoned he might deceive Pegasus into believing that he had given up the pursuit. Naturally the stallion would then slacken his pace, and Pecos could drop down upon his unsuspecting back.

Pecos no sooner thought of this scheme than he put it into execution. He leapt wildly to a beetling cliff, ran swiftly forward, and then leapt down a hundred feet upon the snorting Pegasus.

Pecos Bill had scarcely landed when the startled stallion jumped with arched back high into the air. Pecos Bill flew upward like a skyrocket. Luckily he caught himself by an eyelash in a niche of the jagged rock, several hundred feet above the prancing Pegasus. Otherwise, this calamity might have proved his undoing. As it was, for several minutes Pecos could see groups of flickering stars wherever he happened to look.

Quickly, however, Pecos rubbed the stars out of his eyes, and as he did so the lust of greed burned hotter than ever within his soul. The stallion had, during this time, galloped off down the trail as lightly as if nothing whatever had happened.

The next minute Pecos started leaping wildly down the face of the cliff, and very soon his feet were again firmly treading the trail. He stopped just long enough to send another defiant neigh after the retreating Pegasus.

This last neigh of defiance proved more than the stallion's temper could bear: "Why must I forever run from this puny man-child?" he asked himself. "I'll not run another step; I'll turn and defy him! I'm a hundred times stronger than he is. I'll simply trample him under my feet and teach him manners!"

As he thus assured himself he turned bravely around and planted his forefeet firmly in the trail, which at this place ran narrowly between upright cliffs on either side. He had scarcely a second to wait until Pecos came flying like lightning. Pecos barely avoided a serious collision, for the stallion was standing with every muscle tense, ready to charge down upon him.

"Why, hello, Mr. Pegasus," smiled Pecos blandly in horse language, as he brought himself to a grinding stop.

"Don't you try to Mr. Pegasus me!" the stallion replied enraged. "Have you said your prayers?"

"I say my prayers regularly every morning and evening, though I'll confess they've been brief these past few days, for I've had to say them on the jump," Pecos smiled, showing not the least fear.

Without warning, the angry stallion reared and charged down upon the defenseless man. But Pecos was ready for him. He simply turned a deft air flop and landed prettily on the astonished stallion's back; and before Pegasus could recover from his surprise Pecos Bill had securely fastened his hands in the flying mane and imbedded his clawed toes between the dilating ribs.

From this moment it became a contest between the strength and wits of the horse and the wits and the strength of the man.

At first the stallion tried to run out from under Pecos Bill. Whereupon there ensued an even faster race than the one before—positively the world's record. Pegasus made the first mile in 24 seconds flat. When the horse found that he could not possibly run from beneath Pecos, he began immediately to try to jump out from under him. His first jump was a half mile forward, and his second jump three-quarters of a mile backwards. Pecos, one second, found himself trying to fly over the stallion's ears, and the next second trying to fly over his tail. But in spite of everything, Pecos never quite lost his grip of the horse's ribs and mane.

Very soon there began the greatest bucking contest of all time. Multiply by a thousand the very best that such famous horses of the ranch as Long Tom, Angel, Brown Eyes, Spike, Red Wing, Wiggles, and Flying Devil have ever been able to do, and you have some feeble idea of what was happening now as Pegasus decided to buck Pecos Bill into the middle of the next full moon.

There was *sunfishing,* and *twisting,* and *skyscraping,* and *cake walking,* and *high flying* all at the same thunderous explosive moment. It seemed to Pecos Bill that his day of doom had arrived, but he dared do nothing except hold fast with a life-and-death grip. And he stuck.

When the stallion found he couldn't buck Pecos Bill off his back, he tried rubbing him off by running against trees and rocks. Thus came the most cruel part of the punishment that Pecos was forced to suffer. Had the stallion thought of this earlier, he might possibly have freed himself of Pecos Bill, but now that he was not able to buck or run as hard as at first, Pecos was just able to maintain his hold without the aid of his toes.

In very quick succession Pecos was forced to swing one leg up near the stallion's back and then the other, as the mesquite trees and the sandstone rocks threatened to grind him to a jelly. By the time the furious Pegasus finally gave up, Pecos had all his clothes torn from him and most of his skin was bruised and bleeding.

Then another idea entered the stallion's head: "I'll rear

over backward and crush Pecos under me," he said to himself.

This last effort proved, in the end, the proud stallion's undoing. He woke up the next moment to find Pecos Bill
seated securely on his fore shoulder, with the man's foot
resting heavily on his upturned cheek. Pegasus began to kick
and paw wildly, but the more he struggled the firmer Pecos
came down with his foot.

"Well, Pegasus," Pecos crooned gently in horse language,
"isn't it about time you and me got to be friends? There's
nothing to be gained by our carrying on this fight any longer."

The words sounded like sweet music in the stallion's ear,
but they were so entirely unexpected that he continued to kick
and paw and switch sullenly; but the more he struggled the
more tightly he found himself pinned down.

Pecos Bill held his position firmly and began stroking the
horse's neck tenderly. He also crooned a song of friendship in
language that Pegasus could not fail to understand. After a
time the stallion answered:

"But can I trust you? How do I know that you won't en-
slave me and torture me? . . . I was born to be free like you.
I am used to being my own master. I'll die rather than yield
myself to the slavery of any man!"

"Listen to me, Pegasus," Pecos Bill answered seriously.
"You and I were made for each other. You've got every other
horse in the world beaten a mile; and as for man, I am in a
class all by myself. We can lick everything else in sight.
Listen. We can build up the greatest ranch in all the Southwest range country. Your fame will be sung around the world
for untold generations. You will be known as the Pegasus
among countless thousands of cow ponies!"

"But I'm afraid to trust you! You are a hated *inhuman!*"

Pegasus repeated over and over as he lay prostrate and helpless.

"I'm not what you think. I'm the better part—a noble Coyote. Besides, if you remain here in your wild retreat," Pecos Bill continued, "you will go down unhonored and unsung. Your absolute freedom will lead to a life of idle ease. It will simply mean your undoing. You must remember that no one of all who do the world's work is ever entirely free. Restraint is the price each must pay to duty!"

"You're making a fool of me. I knew it," Pegasus groaned.

"I give you my word of honor, Pegasus," Pecos Bill continued with high seriousness. "If you are loyal to me, I will be loyal to you. If you will but work faithfully with me, the world will very soon be ours!"

With this statement, Pecos Bill freed Pegasus, and the mighty stallion leapt to his feet, shaking himself vigorously. Then he stood stock still for a long minute, undecided whether to run or stay.

"The choice is yours to make, Pegasus," Pecos Bill pleaded. "I'll not take advantage of you, for a spirit such as yours can't be broken. I know, for I myself am a free spirit. You are absolutely free to do as you like. Isn't this proof I'm on the square with you?"

The magnificent white stallion quivered in every muscle. The decision upon which the remainder of his life was to hang was being weighed in the balance. Slowly, at length, Pegasus came and placed his muzzle against Pecos Bill's cheek.

"I will go with you," Pegasus whispered, "wherever you lead."

X.

OLD SATAN BUSTS PIKE'S PEAK

Now that Pecos Bill and Pegasus had found each other, the future of the cattle industry was assured. Mighty deeds were in the offing and no mistake.

During the following day and a half they did some fast traveling. They crossed a large portion of what is today Arizona and New Mexico. Pecos Bill kept in the lead, Pegasus followed closely after. At last they came to the very hillside on the Powder River where Pecos had left his saddle and lariat the morning the great race began.

Pegasus was doubtful at first, but Pecos assured him that there was no danger in a saddle. "Why, any time you get tired of it," Pecos explained, "all you have to do is to arch your back and make one of your *high dives*. Then the girth will rip into a thousand pieces and the saddle itself will fly into the middle of the week after next."

With this assurance on the part of Pecos Bill, Pegasus allowed the girth to be cinched securely; but when it came to having his mouth defiled with a bridle bit, Pegasus was stubborn.

"Very well," Pecos replied, when all his arguments to the contrary had failed, "we'll simply refashion the bridle into a halter. Instead of a bit in your mouth, we'll simply lay the leather across your nose. I will direct you just with the pressure of my knees and the tightening of the reins against your neck. This will be easier for both of us."

With this further agreement, the haughty stallion submitted his head to the halter.

All this while Pecos Bill was in such a fervor of excitement over his success in capturing Pegasus he had entirely failed to notice that all his clothes were torn from him. Now that he was finally in the saddle, he discovered he had reverted to the condition of Cropear, the Coyote. Besides, his shoulders and sides were scratched and bruised shamefully. But he never even slowed up. That wasn't anything. He had Pegasus.

When, however, he noticed that his lariat was still broken, it was a different matter.

"I can never go back to the ranch this way," he confided to Pegasus. "I'll just have to fix up my rope. And I'd better find something to wear. It's not quite customary to go about among *humans* without clothes."

Pecos was undecided what to do next, and Pegasus had no solution to offer. In the middle of this bad fix, Pecos suddenly discovered, at a distance, a great moss-horn steer that looked as ancient as the alkali desert or the jagged hillsides.

Pecos now told Pegasus to stop, tied an improvised noose in his broken lariat, and before the grazing steer was aware that anything was happening, his head was inside the flying rope. The next minute Pecos loosened the hide from behind the steer's ears, grabbed him by the tail, and with a yowl scared the terrified bawling beast so completely that he actually jumped out of his skin.

Meanwhile Pecos braided from the green raw hide a noose for his unfailing lariat.

From the part of the skin that remained Pecos fashioned himself a crude pair of leather breeches, with the hair on the outside, so that he might appear respectable when he reached Hell's Gate Gulch. Thus it was that necessity, as usual, became the mother of invention; for when Pecos grew accustomed to the strange appendages and later told all the cowmen how very serviceable these breeches really were as protection against the rain and the mesquite and cactus thorns, he immediately started a new style. Within a few months leather breeches were all the rage, and no self-respecting cowpuncher dared appear without them. Thus was introduced the strange article of dress that has ever since been called Chaps.

As soon as Pecos had finished repairing his lariat and fashioning his leather breeches, he and Pegasus again started on their way, and the next minute were cutting the air into a long golden ribbon. Before they were quite aware of the distance, they had leapt the high corral fence and were dashing up to the top of Hell's Gate Gulch.

Pecos Bill found the members of the Devil's Cavalry—just as he had expected—squatting on their toes, trying to lay a series of bets on the probability of his actually catching Pegasus. The betting was an entire failure, however, since they all agreed that this particular flying cayuse would never be caught by any mere mortal man.

As Pecos leapt buoyantly down from the magnificent horse, with his lariat over his shoulder, he shouted: "Hello, to you, my merry men!"

The eyes of the Devil's Cavalry were the next minute sticking out so far that Pecos could easily have lassoed them off with his rope. "Well, can't you men believe your senses? I'm Pecos Bill, and this is Pegasus, the Palimino you fellows tried to get your ropes on. Together we're about the handsomest pair of aces you've seen."

"Especially your pants!" roared half a dozen of the men together.

"Give me that ten spot I was just ready to bet you, Shady Biddle!" Old Satan demanded.

Then Old Satan became so charmed with this particular piece of horse flesh just arrived that he forgot all about the bet and just stood there staring at Pegasus. This was indeed the handsomest specimen of cowpony he'd ever laid eyes on. He couldn't quite make up his mind that the stallion was not a sort of heavenly vision. Finally he teetered forward on his toes, rose quickly to his feet and said dreamily, as he twisted his mustache: "I wants to ride your cayuse."

"It's a pleasant afternoon," commented Pecos Bill blandly. "It looks as if we are going to have fair and clearer weather for several days!"

"I said I wants to ride your broncho!" repeated Old Satan,

as he took a step in the direction of the sensitive stallion.

"I said the weather was wonderful," replied Pecos Bill, still more blandly.

"Well, what says you to my humble request?" insisted Old Satan.

"If you'll make your life insurance papers over to me first," smiled Pecos with dry humor, "I'll grant your request."

"I'll give you twenty dollars to boot between your stallion and Baldy Eagle, my best pony. Let me ride him, and if he suits me, I'll give you twenty-five dollars!"

"The horse isn't properly broken in yet," answered Pecos, quietly, "and I don't want anybody to spoil him at this stage in the game!"

"Spoil him!" thundered Old Satan. "Don't you think I knows how to swing a leg across a saddle as well as the best? Ain't I been gentlin' Widow Makers all my life?"

"But Pegasus is a mighty mean horse when he takes the notion," Pecos added. "I give you fair warning!"

Before Pecos could stop him, Old Satan had leapt into the saddle and was raking Pegasus' ribs with his cruel spurs.

From this moment everything happened in such quick succession that no one could afterward describe accurately just what did occur. First there was a violent snort of fury from the stallion and an arched back and a leap like lightning— and then a cloud of dust! A saddle, with a man astride, was seen flying through the air like a charge of shrapnel. About all that the astonished watchers could distinguish was a rapidly disappearing streak of blue that quickly turned to a black blur against the arch of the sky. The stallion remained standing nearby.

By straining their eyes to the limit, Pecos Bill and what

remained of the Devil's Cavalry could just make out the gaunt figure of Old Satan, still astride the saddle, seated on the very tip top of the rocky summit of Pike's Peak.

"He looks about as comfortable as a dilapidated tin rooster weathervane," Sandy Biddle commented between fits of laughter.

"Anybody that can throw a leg across Pike's Peak is some rider! He's captured an everlastin' world's record, I'm tellin' you!" laughed Ace High Ricker.

"The name of that buckaroo ain't Pegasus," shouted Nevada Bunk. "Call him Widow Maker."

"Right you are," chimed in Ace High. "Leapin' Lulu wouldn't be half good enough for this critter. Pecos, you've got to name him Widow Maker!"

"Widow Maker is right," added Shady. "We'll all call him that name from now on!"

"Well, I won't be contrary about it," agreed Pecos Bill. Then, turning to his horse, he talked a while to him in horse language that none of the men understood. After a few minutes the horse seemed to understand and whinnied sweetly. "Yes, now that the horse understands me, I christen him Widow Maker!"

Now that this weighty matter was off their minds, the watchers began to think of a way out of this new dilemma. "The question before the house is," began Shady seriously, "how in thunder is Old Satan to be got out of the middle of this bad fix?"

"You mean, got *down*, idiot!" shouted Ace High. "Don't you know Pike's Peak is twenty thousand feet high, if it's an inch?"

"Better talk of pullin' down the moon or the Pleiades or

the Big Dipper," contributed Nevada. "Old Satan is set for good up there kissin' the stars and duckin' his head once every day to let the moon go by. I'm tellin' you, he's right there to stay!"

"If you'll only wait a minute, I'll see what can be done about it," Pecos Bill commented as he fingered his lariat.

Walking over near where Widow Maker was still standing, Pecos lifted his lariat from his shoulder and began fondling its many coils as if he actually loved them. Then tying a short calf loop, he waved the lariat frantically about his head. With a twist of his wrist and forearm, he sent it flying through the air so fast that no one could possibly see where it was going. After a few minutes, when Pecos Bill felt that the loop had caught over something, he gave a mighty jerk. It was then that the befuddled Old Satan began to fly back to earth, even more rapidly than he had left it a short while before.

When Old Satan finally landed on a pile of granite rock near Pecos' feet, there was a terrific crash. The Devil's Cavalrymen sadly picked up all they found of their senior officer.

At first they feared Old Satan had been killed. But as they listened they could just make out the sound of his heart. Even so, he seemed more like scrambled eggs than anything else, inside his baggy clothes. They picked him up tenderly and placed him on his cot within the ranch house.

They felt carefully of every part of his body, but there didn't seem much that they could do. There were no pieces of his bones long enough to try to set.

After lying there unconscious for three weeks, one day Old Satan simply sat up in bed, opened his eyes, and asked where he was. When Pecos Bill told him what had happened, he smiled sadly.

They picked Old Satan up tenderly

"That's funny," Old Satan said faintly. "At first I thought I was sittin' pretty and ridin' the most wonderful horse in all creation. Then the earth flew out from under me, and after a thousand years I tell you I just set down gently right where the pearly gates was swingin' ajar. I was just gettin' ready for my harp when I felt another yank, and bless me if I wasn't goin' straight down to hell! I guess there wasn't much I'd ever did I wasn't mighty sorry for on that trip. But what happened next's clean out of my mind. All I know is, my ears exploded and my senses went clear to glory."

At the end of six weeks Old Satan had grown an entirely new skeleton and was able to walk about and even brag about his accident. After another fortnight, he was just as well as ever—a little better, if anything.

When Pecos Bill saw how really tough these Devil's Cavalrymen were it came to him like a flash of greased lightning that these were the very cowmen for him to use in starting his proposed ranch.

"But these Cavalrymen are so used to tall talk," Pecos thought to himself, "that I'm afraid what I have to say to them will seem pretty tame and flat. It won't be a bed of roses convincing these dreamers that they'll be better off with me. But here goes."

The next day, while they were all squatting in a circle, each bragging how much tougher he was than Old Satan, Pecos began:

"Gentlemen of the Long Bow, I'm about to leave you. This Hell's Gate Gulch is, in many ways, a pleasant place to live, I'll agree. But it doesn't offer a man any room at all for a life of burning excitement. The trouble is, there isn't a chance here for real action; we haven't got the room to do anything of

any real bigness. When we want a thrill, we've got to go all
the way to Dallas or else ride across the mesa until we find
some lone outrider with a herd of unprotected cattle. What's
that, when you come right down to it? Besides, what is there
to do here in this Gulch except to squat on our toes and tell
tall tales?"

"Pecos, you better remember who you're talkin' to," commented Old Satan, and he wasn't any too polite, the way he
said it, either.

"Please don't get me wrong," Pecos continued. "What I'm
trying to say is simply this: Personally, Widow Maker and I
have got to get straight away from here and out where there's
at least room to take a full breath. That horse and I weren't
meant to be cooped up in any place that's as small and
confining as Hell's Gulch. We're rapid travelers, once we get
going. What we want—and what we're going to get—is some
of that good prairie land and a hundred or so nice, fertile
river valleys that's lying around going to waste because nobody has the nerve. What's the matter with you men? Can't
you remember when these plains were jam-packed with buffalo and antelope?"

"Yes, we do recollect the good old days," mumbled Old
Satan. "But what's that got to do with it? I can't see what difference that would make."

"What I'm about to suggest," added Pecos, smoothly, "is
that it's high time for us to begin to replace the millions of
buffalo with just as many steers or maybe more. Those
Yankees back in New England are just yelling for our western beef. England'll take all she can get. The other states
of Europe are getting thin waiting for it. Who's going to
raise the beef for 'em? We are! What I've got in mind is for

us to go into the cattle business on such a big scale nobody ever saw anything like it before."

"Oh," scoffed Ace High, "you may have caught Widow Maker, Pecos. But that's not sendin' beef to England by a darn sight."

"When we get this proposed ranch rightly started," continued Pecos with growing spirit, "this pigmy valley of yours won't offer sufficient room to shelter the calves that will be born in our herd on a single May morning before breakfast! Why, we'll simply stake off New Mexico for our calf pasture. The Valley of the Rio Grande won't be hardly large enough for one of our smallest herds. We'll crowd the Arkansas Valley with another herd. The Missouri Valley we'll fill as full of cattle as a prairie dog colony's full of houses. Why, I tell you, Canada from coast to coast won't have enough space for the summer overflow from our herds!

"England? Did you say England? Sure, we'll feed her, and we'll feed Germany, France and Italy. We'll get Japan and China so het up about beef, they'll turn up their noses at rice."

"Say, Pecos, how about the moon and the Milky Way?" inquired Old Satan, as he twisted his mustache.

"All the ranches that are now running," continued Pecos Bill, without winking an eyelash, "are small fry compared to what we're going to have. Who says a cowman's rich if he has a thousand steers? We'll have millions, yes, trillions of 'em, if we ever stop to count, which we won't—we'll be too busy."

"You're some talker, Pecos," commented Old Satan with sympathy. "And you know I like nothin' better'n tall talk. But what's botherin' me is how in thunderation you're ever goin' to carry out any such wonders."

"Well, listen and I'll tell you. You, Old Satan, you, Shady, you, Ace High, you, Nevada—all of you Devil's Cavalrymen are going to cut loose and help me. Of course, I wouldn't think of tackling the job alone. I've got to have a good string of cayuses to give me a hand.

"Now listen. What you men need to bring out the real hero that's in you is the chance to help do a real piece of honest-to-goodness hard work. You need the chance to cut loose. The trouble here is that all you can do is to talk big.

"Come with me, my merry cayuses, and each and every one of you will soon be famous. Your names'll be told and your fame sung wherever the taste of beef is sweet upon the tongue. In other words, there won't be a country the sun shines on that won't be talking about you and me too.

"Old Satan, you are going to be the foreman of one of my ranches. The rest of you men'll go to work with him. You're going to swing the long rope and ride the flying broncho.

"We'll make Hell's Gate Gulch into a breeding place for our horses. With Widow Maker the sire for our herd, we'll soon have a breed of bronchos that'll lick the world.

"All you've got to do to put bed rock under this dream is say yes. As soon as you make up your minds to come in with me, the world is ours to walk in anywhere!"

"I'll tell you, Pecos Bill, you and your Widow Maker are as pretty a pair of aces as ever I see," Old Satan smiled dryly. "If there's a chance of me bein' your right bower, I'm right there!"

"Count me in."

"Me too."

"And me."

There wasn't one that held back. The ayes had it.

"That's the stuff," grinned Pecos. "You stay right here, limbering yourselves up on the lasso, and I'll be back as quick as I can from a visit I've got to pay to another string of cayuses I have in mind."

XI.

EYEGLASS DUDE ENGLISHMEN

When Pecos Bill left Hell's Gate Gulch to make a visit to
Pinnacle Mountain Ranch—which was what he had in mind
next—he found that plenty had been going on in his old
crowd.

Gun Smith, Rusty Peters, Moon Hennessey, Mushmouth,
Bean Hole, and all the others were squatting on their toes,
whittling, shooting at targets with tobacco juice, and laying
bets to see who could tell the biggest yarn.

"It's funny," Pecos Bill said to himself as he came up and saw how things were, "here's the same old crimp in the rope. Things going along just too soft. So they have to tell tall tales about how good they are."

"Well, how are things going since I've been away?" he said aloud as he came up quietly behind the men.

"Goin'," laughed Gun Smith, "they're gone!"

"What do you mean?" asked Pecos Bill, looking puzzled.

"Well, we've just sold out everything, and a lot more. When you hear how we cleaned up on a couple of these eyeglass dude Englishmen you'll agree the Devil hasn't anybody slicker'n we are," answered Gun Smith as he lifted his chest high.

"Do tell! Say, you talk just like the Devil's Cavalrymen I've been visiting down at Hell's Gate Gulch. It seems as if idleness locoes everybody alike."

"Well, if you'll agree not to stop me with any more of your burnin' remarks," growled Gun Smith, "I'll tell you what happened."

"Agreed," answered Pecos Bill as he too squatted on his toes and made one of the silent circle.

"Well, when you first left us, Pecos, we was to blame, I suppose. There was so little work to do that we didn't even attend to what there was.

"Things went along like a tune of the heavenly choir for a long while—for six or eight months, I should say. The corral fence was new and as solid as the rock of Gibraltar, and the cattle was too afraid to go up the side of Pinnacle Mountain, or off of it.

"Once in a while, when we was all fed up with settin' around without any more eggs to hatch, we'd maybe ride out daily to see that nothin' had gone wrong.

"But everything was always so perfectly fine that after a while it was just a waste of time, to our way of thinkin', to ride around the twelve miles of fence once a month."

"But don't forget," broke in Chuck, "that all this happened while the fence was so tight a prairie dog wouldn't have been able to find his way through it."

"As I was sayin'," continued Gun Smith, "after a while the old steers got all the grass cropped around the foot of the mountain next the corral. So they just naturally had to crawl higher and higher up Old Pinnacle. We was, by this time, pattin' ourselves so hard on the back that it began to be much worse'n sunburn. With nothin' but just bare stubble between the steers and the fence, we all argued that there wasn't a thing could possibly go wrong. The further they got away from the neighborhood of the fence, the less need there was for us to keep our eye on them. You get the idea, Pecos.

"Well, about this time things begun to get dull, and so we naturally fell to arguin'. We tried to make out which method of picketin' a broncho's the best. Chuck and me held that it's best to hobble the critter's front legs; but Moon Hennessey and his friends held just as strong that the best way's to use the picket rope around the critter's neck.

"Well, day after day, we had it hot and heavy. Moon Hennessey put in his time tryin' to prove that a broncho with his front legs hobbled would jump along with his front feet and walk with his hind feet, and it wasn't anythin' for him to get over at least a dozen miles in a night.

"Chuck and me all the while held fast to our first original point, that it was easier for a broncho to lift a picket stake and get away than it was for him to go hippity-skippity, helter-skelter for any distance.

"After about a month of this talkin' and arguin' we was further apart than we'd been at the start. The only kind of agreement that was left us in the end, was to agree to disagree."

"You've developed the gift of gab while I've been away, Gun Smith," Pecos commented.

"But this wasn't all," Gun Smith continued. "We'd no sooner ended one argument than we got into the middle of another. Moon Hennessey and his crowd took the stand that a wall-eyed white broncho could out-buck all the other critters in creation. Chuck and me then tried to prove that a pinto was the buckaroo that had the biggest bag of tricks.

"Well, this argument lasted the biggest part of another month. And we come out right where we ended up the other time. I mean the only kind of agreement we could reach was to agree to disagree.

"Of course by this time we was most of us feelin' that the fellows opposed to us wasn't usin' any more reason than a stubborn mule. We didn't have the nerve to say what we felt—bein' all worked to such a high pitch of feelin'—or there would've been a free-for-all fight.

"Well, we all got so excited about ourselves that we completely, entirely forgot our bovine charges on Pinnacle Mountain.

"Then one day I begun to get teetotally fed up on battlin' with Moon Hennessey and his string of cayuses. I begun to see that it's easier to remove a mountain the size of Pinnacle than to change a man's mind against his will. So in a day or two I got up from the circle and made up my mind I'd ride around the corral just as a matter of exercise and recreation. I needed a change in scenery all right.

"Well, everything looked fine and dandy for the first four or five miles. I was whistlin' a lively tune and feelin' as saucy as a Blue Jay. Then I thought I saw somethin', and the next minute I was sure that I did. A full mile and a half of that perfectly beautiful fence was completely broke down. The poles and the posts was ground in the dust. It was as flat out as if a cyclone had passed that way!

"Then I looked up the mountain side and couldn't believe my eyes. What I saw was the dents of steers' horns, thousands of 'em, and a hundred or more broken horns themselves scattered everywhere. Next I looked down the valley, and a couple of miles away I saw a swarm of vultures that nearly pulled my eyes out—as many as five or ten thousand, it seemed. I'd have bet my best lariat I had a whiff of somethin' that didn't smell exactly like wild flowers.

"I couldn't make it out at all. So I got down off my broncho and walked up the side of the mountain to make a careful examination. I could still see the dents the steers had made in the mountain. And when I got up higher I could see where the stampede'd started. It was like the mowers leavin' off their last swath right at that exact spot. Down below, the mountain was as bare as my hand; up above it was covered with rank bunch grass not eaten, tramped down or anythin'.

"But I wasn't satisfied yet so I climbed higher and looked everywhere. Then I got on to what had happened, all right. A bald eagle had swooped down to pick up a jack rabbit. Mr. Rabbit had seen him comin' and was too smart on his feet to be caught sittin' still. I could see distinctly where the tussle had been carried on. Here the eagle had clawed up a clump of bunch grass; here he had swooped down in the dust; and here a short distance away, lay a neat pile of bones.

The stampede down the mountain side

"When the eagle had at last caught him, Mr. Rabbit had let out such a squeal of fright that the old roan steer nearest him was scared into a sudden panic and started at breakneck speed. He hadn't taken more than three jumps when he lost his balance and started to roll head over heels down the mountain, and of course his horns tore up the turf every time they struck. This naturally started a stampede among the other fool steers, and in less than a minute the entire side of the mountain wasn't anythin' but flyin' horns and tails.

"Say, I'd have given a million dollars to have seen them thousand steers tumblin', their crazy tails flappin' like lariats, and their horns glistenin' every which way. I can't think of a single sight I'd rather have seen than just that!

"But by the time I found them, they was too far gone to save even their skins; just a total loss, that's what.

"After I'd doped it all out I rode back to the ranch house faster than my pony'd ever gotten me there before and yelled, 'Fire! Murder!' and everythin' else that came into my mind. The men tumbled out of the shack quicker'n it takes to tell it. It's always that way of course, you close the gate after the steer is stolen.

"But this wasn't the worst. When the steers that happened at the time to be on the opposite side of the mountain found the fence down they made for the tall timber and the sage brush without losin' a minute.

"If it hadn't been for one thing we'd have lost every last steer of the entire herd. The cows, you see, couldn't go, for they couldn't take their calves along. The calves themselves couldn't go because they had all been born with a short pair of legs on the side next the mountain. This all came about through their mothers lookin' at the mountainside menagerie

day after day—at the Dodo birds and the rabbits with two
short legs next the mountain, and the rest of 'em. Somewhere
or other I heard tell how a man set up before the cattle of
his father-in-law, rods of green poplar which he had made
ring-streaked, spotted and speckled, and before you knew it
the father-in-law had nothing but ring-streaked, spotted and
speckled calves. It's funny about cattle that way, but it's true,
all right.

"We was glad to see that a good many steers had stayed behind with the cows and their slim-legged calves. And soon
we was scoutin' about everywhere lookin' for our lost cattle.
We rounded up all the stragglers we could find, until we had
on Pinnacle Mountain about an even thousand head of steers.

"Bein' without your knack of carryin' on a talk with the
prairie dogs, Pecos, we hadn't any way of gettin' over to 'em
the idea that we wanted 'em to dig a fresh supply of post
holes. Nothing for it but to do it ourselves anyway. So we
slaved and sweat over that fence for six weeks. We sure was
mad with ourselves, not mentionin' bein' fed up with Pinnacle Mountain, for we was findin' out there ain't no such
thing as a Perpetual Motion Ranch. If you'd been here, Pecos,
to boss the work on the new fence it would've been all right.

"At last when we was all through, and had what was left
of the herd back on their range again, we set down and argued
for a week as to which is the biggest fool: the steer that allows
itself to be stampeded over nothin', or the steer that allows
itself to go crazy over the taste of the loco weed.

"We was just in the middle of the hottest debate we'd ever
staged with no hint at an agreement, when we was stopped
by two of these eyeglass dude Englishmen. They said they'd
heard we owned a very wonderful ranch, don't ye know,

don't ye know! And they screwed their monocles this way and that, and they played with their watch fobs, and they played with their 'aitch's.' They said they'd come a thousand miles through wild country to find us.

"Yes, we told 'em they hadn't heard the half of the wonders of our ranch. We let them know that ours was the only successful perpetual motion ranch that had ever been invented in all the history of cowmen. The thing ran itself. All you needed to do was to set down and whittle and swap yarns—the bigger the yarns were, the better—and all the while the cattle was takin' perfect care of themselves.

"All the work had already been done by God. For a fact. We told 'em so. He'd furnished every sort of climate that any kind of bovine critter could ever desire. He had planted enough grass to last until the day after the last steer would eat his fill. We praised Old Pinnacle up one side and down the other. And I don't know how many times we said this was the only ranch of its kind in the world and that there never could be no other ranch like it, since there wasn't no other mountain like Pinnacle. Why, we proved that we could raise beef here for an average of less than one-sixteenth cent a pound. By marketin' the steers for five cents a pound, we was makin' a clear profit of eight thousand per cent.

"So, you see, you can't exactly blame those eyeglass dude Englishmen for askin' if our Pinnacle Ranch was for sale.

"You can't blame us either if we hemmed and hawed for half a day, tellin' them the thought of sellin' was entirely contrary to our wishes. Old Pinnacle was such a wonderful gold mine that we couldn't think seriously of givin' it up.

"When we'd worked them up to just the right pitch of bein' crazy to buy it, we told 'em we might take five dollars apiece for each steer in the herd, and throw in Old Pinnacle as a sort of donation.

"Well, the dudes thought this a great bargain till they come to ask us how many head of steers we had in the herd. We showed them the books to prove that we had fifteen hundred calves. And then we proved to them that a herd contained five times as many cattle as there was calves. That would make our ranch number seven thousand five hundred.

"The dude Englishmen twisted their monocles and their watch fobs and did some rapid figurin'. Then the oldest and the most dudish of the two said: 'Before we'll pay you thirty-seven thousand five hundred dollars, don't you know, we'll have to count your cattle to make sure we're gettin' what we pay for.'

"We told them as politely as possible that this wasn't exactly the way things was done in this neck of the woods, that whenever anybody wanted to buy a ranch he took the books as proof that the cattle were all there.

"But accordin' to English methods of doin' business, don't you know, by Jove, they'd have to take a count of our steers.

"So, you see, there the matter hung for a whole long day. Then Chuck whispered somethin' in my ear while the English dudes was admirin' the landscape, and I smiled and told them, while they screwed their monocles some more, that we was willin' that they should make the count. We was, of course, put out that they should doubt our word, but since they was not used to the laws of the range country, and since it was purely a matter of business, we'd concede a point and let the sale go through.

"Of course, we started in with the calves, as we was sure we could make them believe we had the number that our books showed. So we set the English dudes at a certain station and told them we'd drive our calves past.

"The oldest dude stood and counted and the other marked little lines and crosses in his book with a lady's gold-mounted pencil. We scattered the calves in a line reachin' all the way 'round the mountain, and then we started the procession revolvin' till they'd counted fifteen hundred. The calves with their short legs next the mountain walked so downright elegant the dudes never suspected they had to lean against a tree to sleep at night. Once they laid down, they couldn't for the life of them get up again.

"After the calves was counted, we took the dudes a lot higher up where the distance around was a great deal shorter, and strung our herd out until the steers, too, formed a circle as complete as one of the rings of Saturn. We was all puffin' and wheezin', and holdin' our breaths for fear somethin' would happen. For all these English dudes is so green, they might possibly find out what we was doin', if everythin' didn't move like clock work.

"Well, everythin' went O. K. the first two or three hours. The steers marched past like tin soldiers. I stood beside the old eyeglass dude to make sure he didn't miss his count.

"Everythin' would've been as smooth as silk if it hadn't been for one old roan steer with a big, sprawly patch of white down his rump. He was so old there was frost on his beard and his face was wrinkled like a dried apple peel. He was lop-horned and bob-tailed. He had a terrible limp in his front pastern. He was a critter any cattleman could have picked out of a herd of a million steers a mile away. We'd nicknamed him Old Jonah, and we would've shot him if we hadn't been so sorry for him.

"Well, about the tenth time Old Jonah come limpin' past in his turn, my lord Gentleman squinted a little harder through his monocle and said: 'There are more no account, blarsted lop-horned, crippled roan brutes in this herd than anythin' else, don't you know.'

" 'But, my lord,' replied the other dude as he kept right on markin' the numbers without lookin' up from his book, 'this sort of cow'll do very fine for tinned devil'd ham to feed the soldiers.'

"The oldest dude raised his chest and growled somethin' about the woeful ignorance of the younger generation when it come to any practical knowledge of cattle and swine, of bully beef and tinned ham, and then went on with his countin' like he was wound up.

"I signaled to Chuck, when the dudes wasn't lookin', tc cut out Old Jonah from the line of march before he'd the chance to come around again. On the other side of Old Pinnacle the men tried every way to stop the doggoned brute without startin' a stampede; but in spite of all they could do, Old Jonah kept right on with his march.

"About the fifteenth time around the old dude turned and said to me: 'By the way, Boss, how many of these old roan lop-horns does your herd contain?'

" 'I don't know exactly,' says I, gingerly, 'but they don't run higher than one to every four or five hundred at the very most. Of that I'm absolutely sure.'

" 'You can hardly expect a business man of my standin' to pay you five dollars apiece for such critters, don't you know.'

" 'Suit yourself,' I answers as sweet as a canary bird. 'We'll throw in all the lop-horned roans for good measure. You needn't include them in your count.'

"When I said that, you should've seen the old dude's chest raise. It went up at least six inches to think of the hard bargain he was drivin' with a poor ignorant, woolly Wild West American cowpuncher.

" 'That's very white of you, don't you know,' he says, screwing in his monocle. Then without movin' a muscle, he sings out over his shoulder to that other dude: 'Strike out twenty-seven for an overcount.'

"Well, our steers kept on a-marchin' round and round until they was so tired and footsore they couldn't hardly lift a leg. I begun to lose hope that we'd ever be able to keep 'em going long enough to make out the count we'd promised. But Old Jonah was faithful to the last. Round and round, round and round, round and round. He never missed a count.

"After we'd sweat blood for three or four hours longer, we finally made our count to satisfy the dudes. And we was singin' hallelujahs under our breath. No mistake about it.

"Then just as we was leavin' the place and all the other steers had laid down to rest, here come Old Jonah round again all by himself.

" 'That old lop-horn looks strangely familiar,' sings out the old dude.

" 'Yes, these steers of the older generation all were given the same kind of schoolin',' I explained in schoolbook language imported for the occasion. 'The lessons life teaches them are all alike, don't you know. And so, by Jove, you can't exactly blame them for all lookin' as alike as jackrabbits, or prairie dogs, or mockin' birds.'

" 'But just the same,' replied my lord with another twist of his monocle, 'these old brutes somewhat offend my artistic sense of the fitness of things. Here amidst all this beauty comes ugliness. It's all deucedly grotesque, and out of place, don't you know.'

" 'But, my lord,' sings out the young dude, 'these very ancient ones are the first we shall put into tin. When they're shipped back to Old England, the sailors will think this the best of American—what the deuce do you call it—devil'd—er —bully beef!'

"Well, that night after we'd closed our deal with the great and glorious Old World business men and had given them a liberal discount of five per cent for cash, we was nervous wrecks. I was so worked up that I couldn't sleep. All I could see was a procession of lop-horned roan steers with white rumps, goin' past me in a single file—round and round, round and round.

"Wasn't any use tryin' to sleep, so I got up and wandered out across the slope of Pinnacle Mountain. And would you believe it, there Old Jonah was still a-pacin' round and round the mountain. He'd got started and had got the habit and couldn't stop. I watched him go by a dozen times and then come back to bed.

"Believe it or not, next day Old Jonah was still goin' round and round. His eyes was set and his feet seemed to be movin' without him knowin' it.

"Pecos, I'm tellin' you God's truth, Old Jonah kept right on millin' round and round for a full week. If you don't believe it, I can take you up and show you the path he wore doin' it. Then the next thing we knowed, Old Jonah dropped dead in his tracks.

"Now the boys is all afraid to go out-of-doors after dark. Moon Hennessey and Chuck has both reported seein' Old Jonah's ghost still pacin' round and round, round and round, with the same doggone motion and the same stare in his eyes."

When Gun Smith had finished, Pecos Bill laughed loud and long: "It serves the smarties right! The conceited monkeys! And to think they can come out here and beat us at our own game, *don't you know!*"

"Them one-eyed Eastern dudes don't know a woodpecker from a blue jay, nor a prairie dog from a porcupine," added Moon Hennessey in disgust.

"But where are these dudes now?" asked Pecos Bill, curiously.

"Oh, they've gone off somewhere to fetch their bags and baggage. They're due to be back here day after tomorrow. Then's when we give 'em possession of Pinnacle and of Old Jonah's ghost!" chirped Gun Smith.

"You know," said Pecos abruptly, "I've got to go off on a little jaunt of my own. You men keep right on with your fun and I promise you I'll be back to see you turn over the property to my lord and his chief Dog Robber."

"Seems to me you gad about a lot more'n you should," commented Gun Smith.

"But it can't be helped," answered Pecos. "I've got another ranch waiting for you fellows that'll make Pinnacle Mountain look like a stunted wart," he laughed as he took his leave with great speed.

Then without the men's even suspecting, Pecos Bill guided Widow Maker across the mesa and through the mesquite woods and along the river valleys, until he had brought together a herd of cattle more than large enough to make up the number the dude Englishmen thought they were buying. He soon had these safely rounded up and inside the corral fence without being seen by a single one of his men. When he had finished, he smiled at Widow Maker, then he said:

"It isn't quite according to my notion of what's square to cheat even a dupe of a conceited English dude."

XII.

ENTER SLUE-FOOT SUE

An hour before the eyeglass Englishmen were due to take possession of Pinnacle Mountain, Pecos returned. He found Gun Smith and the others squatting on their toes just as he had left them, whittling and exchanging tall talk and arguing.

"This is my plan for our future," Pecos began abruptly as soon as he entered and coming at once to the point. "We're going to start the most tremendous, the biggest and the best ranch ever thought up by the mind of man. The

valleys of the Missouri, the Arkansas, the Rio Grande, and
the Platte will not begin to hold our millions of steers, after
we get rightly going. The fact is, our cattle will pasture all
the way from the wild mountain plateaus of central Mexico
to the eternal snows of northern Canada."

"You don't say!" gasped Gun Smith.

"What brand of squirrel whiskey you been drinkin'?"
scoffed Moon Hennessey.

"You yourselves," continued Pecos rapidly, "still remember
when all these valleys were as full of buffalo as the sea is with
water. We are now going to fill these same valleys with steer.
We are going to produce at least one steer for every buffalo
that has been killed."

"Are you sure you ain't been drinkin' somethin' stronger
than water, or eatin' the locoweed?" Bean Hole now inquired
with a puzzled grin. "You don't sound quite sober to me."

"You cowboys are about to write your names on the death-
less scroll of fame," Pecos added in a hurry. "Men the world
over will rise up and call you great and wonderful because
you had the foresight to furnish them with delicious beef. In
England and in France and in Germany, yes, and in Italy and
Russia, and even in Japan and China, men will soon be living
on the food we furnish."

"You shouldn't exactly include England, *don't you know!*"
laughed Moon Hennessey. "Them two dudes that is takin'
charge of Old Pinnacle later today is goin' to keep the British
Lion so stuffed with *tinned beef* that he won't be able to
growl."

"Ours is a chance that comes to the world only once in a
hundred—or better still, a thousand—years," continued Pecos
unruffled. "You are all coming with me this very afternoon,

and together we will work miracles. These valleys of the un-peopled West will be made to blossom as the rose!"

"Say, Pecos, you don't sound at all like yourself. Are you perfectly sure somebody hasn't been treatin' you to some Indian fire water? Or else that you ain't been eatin' locoweed?" Gun Smith asked seriously.

It was no wonder that the men were all surprised, for this was the first time they had ever heard Pecos Bill use such fancy words. He'd never been so solemn before, either. He was talking just as if it was up to him to save the cow country.

"There are still countless herds of wild cattle roaming about wherever one happens to travel," added Pecos. "We will collect these and brand them. If there is need for larger numbers, after these are rounded up, we will go out into the open market and buy as many additional steers as we need with the money we are getting from the sale of Pinnacle Mountain."

By this time the men were so staggered by Pecos Bill's scheming they hadn't a word to say. He was just locoed. He needn't think he'd get them into any such monkey business.

"This afternoon, after the present business is settled, we will all go back to our old I. X. L. Ranch, and from that base start our new business," Pecos continued, quite unaware of the mutiny that was gathering force within the minds of his men.

The situation, however, was quickly relieved by the arrival of my lord and his train of camp followers. Pack horses extended in a line as far as the eye could see. They were undoubtedly bringing the most impossible collection of useless house furniture that had ever been assembled in the state of Texas. There were the best beds and the most costly mattresses. There were chairs of all sorts and descriptions, and fancy lace curtains, and sets of Old English china!

"Won't the Texas fleas we're leavin' behind find a paradise inside them mattresses?" scoffed Moon Hennessey.

What had already appeared was nothing, however, to the excitement that came with the arrival of the two women! And no wonder, for this was positively the first time in the history of the state of Texas that Pecos and Gun Smith and the rest had ever heard of gentlewomen trying to live on a ranch. And one of them a beauteous young lady, at that.

My lord arrived in high spirits, screwed his monocle and announced: "Oh, yes, by Jove, here we are, don't you know."

"So we perceive," answered Pecos Bill with easy dignity.

A moment later the women entered and my lord continued: "This is the place—don't you think it deucedly quaint?"

Pecos and Gun Smith and the other men snatched off their five-gallon hats and swallowed their tongues. They stood nervously fidgeting through a long silence, and then Slue-foot Sue, the beauteous young lady aforesaid, began suddenly to chatter:

"Oh, Mother, I have never been quite so excited in all my born life! Look! They even wear hairy pantaloons and jingly spurs and real guns that shoot bullets, and hats big enough to cover the moon, and everything else we've read about! Why, I just can't wait till I can jump into cowboy clothes myself. Won't I look gorgeous, though, when I hop on a real wild Texas broncho! Oh, it will be simply adorable. I haven't been so excited since the day I rode the Catfish down the Rio Grande with only a surcingle."

During this time my lord had drawn a silk handkerchief from his breast pocket and had dusted a bench for his wife. Now she sat down weakly, so overcome by her daughter's daring she could scarcely speak. "Sue, you shock me to death!

Sue dancing about the shack floor

Your father and I will see that you remain dressed properly
as becomes a gentlewoman!"

By this time my lord had also dusted off a bench for himself
and had sat down gingerly lest he might spot his tweeds.
Slue-foot Sue paid not the least attention to her severe parents.
She was like an uncorked bottle of ginger ale. She danced
about the shack floor, clapped her hands, kicked up her heels,
and began to sing a song she'd learned on the way up the
mountainside:

> "As I was a-walkin' one morning for pleasure
>   I spied a cowpuncher all ridin' along;
> His hat was throwed back and his spurs was a-jinglin',
>   As he approached me a-singin' this song:
>
> " 'Whoopee! tu yi yo, git along, little dogies,
>   It's your misfortune and none of my own,
> Whoopee ti yi yo, git along, little dogies,
>   For you know that Texas will be your new home.' "

As soon as the lively girl had finished, she looked sharply about the circle of gaping cowboys and said glibly: "I say,
Mr. Cowboy—I mean you with the shiny eyes and the red
hair and the big boots—how much will you charge to give
me a course of lessons in broncho riding? I've already had
saddle lessons in London. . . . And I've ridden Catfish in the
Rio Grande and a few little things like that; but your wild
cowponies are entirely different. I can tell by your looks that
you're the one boy who knows exactly how a broncho should
be ridden."

When Slue-foot Sue said "big boots," all the men wanted to
laugh aloud. It seemed the girl was ignorant of the cowboy
customs! So their faces remained as hard as bronze and Pecos

Bill himself blushed so hard that the crimson showed plainly through his tanned skin. He replied in a confused manner that gave his men the keenest enjoyment:

"Well, as soon as your mother and your father give their consent to your wearing a buckskin shirt and chaps—excuse me, er, I mean—of course, I wouldn't want to charge you a cent—as I was saying—of course, I'm busy today—but another time—I'll return after you are all settled and have nothing else to worry about."

"Upon my word!" Slue-foot Sue chirped again, as she looked at the tense, uncomfortable cowmen. "Why, the books didn't say a word about real alive cowpunchers being more bashful than school boys! Upon my word, I can scarcely believe my eyes!"

Without waiting for a reply she clapped her hands joyously, stamped her foot, kicked her wild heels about the rough floor, singing:

"Sing 'er out, my bold Coyotes! leather fists and leather throats,
    Tell the stars the way we rubbed the haughty down.
We're the fiercest wolves a-prowling and it's just our night for
        howling—
        Ee-Yow! a-riding up the rocky trail from town!"

While Sue was singing her mother rose stiffly and spoke in high-pitched reproof: "Sue, child! Wherever did you learn such terrific songs! Stop, I say. Cease immediately!"

"I'm sorry, Mother dear," the excited girl answered, "but when I'm feeling like this there's nothing in the world can stop me! But what harm is there in feeling the way I do now? I'm in the most wonderful country on earth!"

It was thus that Slue-foot Sue suddenly made her way into the minds and hearts of the men.

Soon my lord beckoned Pecos Bill, Gun Smith and the others out into the shack kitchen, and there gave them the money for the Pinnacle Mountain ranch. As soon as this was finished, Pecos Bill and Gun Smith wished my lord the best of luck with his new venture, and then set out for the I. X. L. ranch.

As the men rode along their way they were green-eyed to think that Slue-foot Sue should have chosen Pecos Bill to teach her to ride. But they hadn't forgotten what she had called him.

Gun Smith started the ball rolling: "Big Boots, what is the color of your sweet little horsewoman's hair and eyes?"

"You can call them any color you like," Pecos Bill answered with a broad smile. "The joke is on you fellows, whatever their color may be. I can see, with half an eye, that you're all as jealous as a nest of Porcupines. I'm the man—thanks to my large understanding—who is to teach the most wonderful woman in Texas or the Southwest to ride the loping cow-horse!"

"Yes—er—" Gun Smith retorted in imitation of Pecos Bill's earlier confused reply to Slue-foot Sue, " 'scuse me—I mean, er—I was sayin'—today I'm busy—but—I'm a wonderful Romeo!"

When Gun Smith ended his speech, the mesa resounded loud and long with laughter. And then, as the men rode forward, chap rubbing friendly chap, they started to argue seriously over the color of Slue-foot Sue's hair and eyes. The fact was, had it been known, they had all been so badly scared at the time they had the chance to look at the girl, that they had observed nothing accurately. They could not have told—had their lives depended upon their report—anything definite about a single one of Slue-foot Sue's features. All the time they were arguing every man was seeing in Slue-foot Sue the girl of his dreams.

Very soon Gun Smith and Chuck decided that she was a perfect pinto maverick, and Moon Hennessey and his follow-ers decided just as positively that she was a wall-eyed albion broncho. The longer and hotter the debate waxed the more each was sure that he was absolutely right.

Pecos Bill kept entirely out of the argument. Only once did he speak, and that was when Moon Hennessey recklessly used a disrespectful word in referring to Slue-foot Sue. Then his hand instantly found the butt of his gun and he said coolly:

"Moon, take that back! You're entirely wrong, and you know it!"

Moon Hennessey's face went white in anger, then slowly relaxed.

"I did say what I didn't know," he answered slowly.

"You know you did, and we all know it," added Pecos Bill very quietly.

The other men pretended to take no notice of the occur-rence. Mushmouth started a rollicking song, playing his lip-piano with one side of his mouth and singing the words with the other. The matter was dropped immediately. Moon Hen-nessey, however, had been publicly disgraced and began to nurse again his old grudge against his leader—a grudge that was to grow more bitter with the passing of time.

As he continued riding leisurely in the lead, Pecos Bill was, for the first time in his life, being plagued with unreal fancies. Wherever he directed Widow Maker, or whichever way he looked, he saw before him a pair of roguish, sparkling, danc-ing eyes, and heard a liquid voice that he said to himself was like clear water in a mountain brook, breaking over white pebbles. Just around the next curve in the trail he kept coming upon the gleam of sparkling blue eyes with an aura of burnished gold.

However hard he tried, Pecos could not shake this vision of beauty from him. Even when he later tried to sleep, he seemed ever pursuing, against his better judgment, Slue-foot Sue, who was riding a Catfish down a wide river faster than he could swim. She would dart into the most dangerous current and for the instant completely vanish. She was taunting and luring him despite his will. What had suddenly happened was that Pecos Bill, greatest cowboy of them all, had fallen head over heels in love.

Just as they were finally reaching the I. X. L. ranch shack, Gun Smith put an end to all future arguments concerning Slue-foot Sue.

"If we hadn't o' been quite so greedy in cheatin' the Old Dude, some of us could go back to Pinnacle Mountain. We could pretend that we'd left behind a pair of big boots or somethin' even more valuable, say a surcingle the size to fit a catfish! But as matters now stand between us and the owner of the Perpetual Motion Ranch, we'd best be mighty careful even about whisperin' the name of Old Pinnacle or of sayin' anything to anyone about the place. Somebody from His Majesty's Kingdom will likely be wantin' to hang most of us to the nearest tree. And you can't blame my lord in the least if he actually tries to do it! Take my advice. Spend your time talkin' about somethin' else. Never mention the old Dude or his pinto maverick again as long as you live!"

"Your advice is excellent—that is, as far as you are all concerned," added Pecos Bill with decision.

"But you are a law unto yourself, I infer!" snarled Moon Hennessey.

"The affair at Pinnacle Mountain is closed!" replied Pecos Bill.

To Widow Maker, however, Pecos whispered smilingly: "Honesty is sure on our side in this deal. Aren't we glad now that we filled Pinnacle Mountain with more steers than Slue-foot Sue's father paid us for!"

XIII.

CUTTING PEE-WEE'S EYE TEETH

Gun Smith and his string of men very soon learned that the running of a ranch on anything like the scale of Pecos Bill's ambition was not entirely child's play. The fact was that Pecos had already rounded up so many stray cattle his men were worked almost to death. Things were popping from the minute at early dawn when Bean Hole shouted, "Roll out! you sleepy beggars! Come and take it, or I'll throw it out in the slop!" Until they were safely at rest on their pallets at long after midnight, there was not a single idle minute. They were often in the saddle twenty-seven hours a day and seventeen days a week. There were always cattle and more cattle!

Pecos Bill was absent for days at a time. He had started other ranches—though his men did not know it—and had to share his time among them.

With this state of affairs the cowpunchers found it necessary to make their own amusement; for without a little fun they would have broken under the strain. Practical jokes became the order of the day. And woe betide any innocent greenhorn who happened to apply for work in their midst.

If the greenhorn showed a true sense of humor and if he took no offense, but entered heartily into the horse play, he was likely to get off fairly easy. If, however, a know-it-all, who pretended that he was bridle wise when he wasn't, came bragging into camp that he had seen the elephant and had talked with the owl, then the real fun began.

It so happened one evening while Pecos Bill was away that the men saw a stranger approaching on foot. They were, at the time, gathered about the chuck wagon eating their supper. While he was still half a mile away their sharp eyes detected that he was a breezy young man who gave evidence by every movement that he was away from home for the first time. As he came nearer they saw instantly that he had on a new suit of mail order cowboy clothes. He was carrying himself with a swagger, very evidently entirely convinced that he was making an impression. He carelessly dangled his cigarette loosely between his lips in a way that made the cowpunchers think him a dude.

"What do you think," called Moon Hennessey, pretending he was trying to conceal what he was saying from the approaching stranger, "is it a blue jay or a robin?"

"It ain't yet growed enough tail feathers to be a jay," commented Chuck with assumed sagacity, "and it ain't got quite neat enough clothes to be a robin!"

"It's more like a Pee-wee," added Gun Smith pleasantly between huge bites of boiled cow. "Sounds and looks exactly like that sort of retirin' creature."

The stranger had heard all that was being said and immediately showed his dislike for such childish humor: "Oh, I know your little game, all right!"

"Now it's got out its hammer," continued Gun Smith coolly. "I guess it's got a drop or two of woodpecker's blood in its veins somewhere. But not enough to do it any harm, for it's plain to see, after all, it's only an ordinary complainin' Pee-wee."

"What I want to know without any more fooling," interrupted the stranger, quite out of patience, "is whether I can sleep here tonight."

"Now I know for sure it's a whinin' Pee-wee!" Gun Smith announced decisively. Then turning politely to the stranger, he added, "What was it you was wishin' to communicate, Mr. Pee-wee?"

"I was just asking whether I could *bunk* with you tonight!" the stranger repeated in a tone of sarcasm. He showed his growing impatience by the way he put his cigarette nervously to his mouth and by the way he tilted his chin and blew the smoke through his nose.

"Bunk!" Gun Smith replied, with perfect good manners. "I never heard tell of that particular critter. Is he a blood relation of the Prairie Dog? Oh, yes, I do seem to remember hearin' that he was a twin cousin to the Skunk. But, my friend, all I can say is that you got me guessin'."

"Sleep, then," exploded the stranger as he threw his cigarette to the ground and crushed it beneath his heel.

"Oh, well, now that you've chewed it finer, I begin to understand you," replied Gun Smith in the best of humor. "It's a place to sleep you're drivin' at, is it? I'm really very sorry to be obliged to tell you that we have no time to sleep around this ranch. The nearest we ever come to it is when we drop off into a cat nap for a few minutes every week or two. Of course, you won't understand how dangerous it is around here, and so, of course, you won't realize why we don't dare to sleep, even if we had the chance." And then, suddenly changing to a very serious tone of voice, he asked: "By the way, my friend, are you acquainted with the Wouser?"

"What is it, something good to eat?" queried the stranger, showing himself a smart Aleck.

"I see that my first impression of you was quite correct. You're only a complainin' Pee-wee," Gun Smith went on seriously. "You evidently ain't got the slightest acquaintance with the Texas wilderness. Wousers are a cross between a Mountain Lion and a Grizzly Bear—or that's what they look like, only they are three times bigger'n a long-horned steer. Why, they take two men at a single meal and think no more about it than as if they were feedin' on bunch grass. And so, you see, one of us has to be responsible for keepin' the Wousers away while the others take a short cat nap. He has to keep his trigger finger awake all night long."

"That sounds reasonable," answered the stranger with increasing respect for what was being said to him.

"Another of us's got to keep off the Tarantulas," continued Gun Smith, as sober as a judge, "and still another's accountable for guardin' off the Rattlesnakes. Still another of us has to keep his ear open for the first sound of the stampedin' herd. Then there's the Skunks and the Porcupines. One of the boys has to go around—whenever anybody begins to snore—and close his mouth so that the Leaping Lizards won't jump down his throat. Then there's the Gilaopolis that's bigger'n a yearlin' calf and has a feverish breath so hot he can melt all the solder off our tomato cans. Yes, and about the worst of 'em all is the Hellidad that looks like a cross between a Zebra and a Ostrich. His particular desire is to lick you bald-headed while you slumber. So you see, Mr. Pee-wee, a cowboy takes his life literally out of his own hands when he allows himself to do more'n take a light cat nap!"

"But you haven't answered my question," the stranger replied in a very changed tone of voice.

"I don't know as we object. We're a little crowded here for sleepin' quarters, as you see," Gun Smith drawled as he pointed to the four corners of the out-of-doors. "But we can manage somehow to find room to spread you a pallet, I suppose. You won't object to lyin' between two of us ol' flea-bitten critters, will you? We make it a rule here never to leave a stranger to himself, for he is pretty sure to forget and fall into a deep sleep. Then by the time we get him awake agin it's too late and the damage has gone beyond repair."

"That's what happened last month to that Mr. Percival Lowell Snodgrass we had with us from Massachusetts. Stranger, you can see his grave over there now. A big bull Rattlesnake took him a nip on the wrist," added Moon Hennessey with mock seriousness.

By this time Mr. Pee-wee was beginning to be visibly nervous. He was only too glad to get the chance to lie between Gun Smith and Chuck.

Later in the evening, after all were stowed away safely for the night, things began to happen.

Gun Smith pretended to fall asleep immediately. He stretched himself, mumbled something which sounded as if he were terribly tired, and within a few minutes he began to snore. Making believe not to awaken him, Chuck reached over quietly and closed his mouth.

Within a few minutes his mouth was wide open again and he was puffing like a winded bull maverick on a stiff grade.

Then before Chuck could reach him again, Gun Smith made believe he was choking. He sat up, let out a suppressed shriek, and began struggling with something that seemed caught in his throat. He had a piece of rawhide ready for the occasion and in the moonlight this looked to Mr. Pee-wee strangely like a Leaping Lizard. Finally Gun Smith dislodged it, jumped up and ran a few paces away from the others and pretended to vomit violently.

"I'll be makin' the old fool a halter to keep his mouth shut if this keeps up," growled Moon Hennessey. "What does he think he is, keepin' the rest of us awake like this?"

When Gun Smith came back he proceeded to tell everybody, in no unmistaken language, what he thought of such a lizard-infested state as Texas.

"Shut up, you blatherin' idiot," shouted Mushmouth, pretending to be as mad as a hornet. "Don't you know the rest of us can't sleep while you're yowlin' around, you old catamount! We'll be makin' you a halter tomorrow, sure!"

"Another word, an' I'll throw out the first fellow who says it," growled Chuck. "Gun Smith, you lay down again and keep your old fool mouth shut."

Mr. Pee-wee could hear him panting and gagging and still

*"The Hellidad's particular desire is to lick you bald-headed
while you slumber"*

cursing Lizards under his breath. Mr. Pee-wee's hands were by this time clasped over his own mouth as tight as a vise.

Everything for the minute was so quiet that Mr. Pee-wee could hear his heart thumping a mile a minute. He had never known what it was to be scared. But he did now.

Thus things dragged on for nearly an hour—an hour that seemed at least three or four months to the frightened tenderfoot. Then across the silence there came a most unearthly shriek. It simply curdled Pee-wee's blood. It sounded to him like the despairing wail of a dying man and the yowl of a Grizzly Bear. Nobody stirred for a minute, during which the tenderfoot shivered in an ague of fear. Again the same cry resounded, but very much nearer.

Needless to say, it was Mushmouth, who had sneaked away when no one was watching and was now running toward the spot where the men lay, making these unearthly noises.

When the third shriek sounded but a few rods away, Gun Smith and Chuck sat up suddenly. Both grabbed the tenderfoot and shook him hard as they shouted: "Up! Up! It's the Wouser!"

They grabbed their guns and fired four or five distinct volleys high in the air. Again came the blood-curdling shriek, now but a few yards away. Following this immediately came another volley of gun fire, which brought a howl of pain and then prolonged silence.

Everybody rushed over in the direction of the sound and Gun Smith spoke loud enough to be heard for half a mile: "Upon my life, it's the biggest Wouser we've seen this year. Bullfrog Doyle, you and Chuck stand guard. His mate'll be around any minute now, and if we ain't mighty careful he'll sure carry one or more of us away!"

A few minutes later, when they began to look around for Mr. Pee-wee, they could find no trace of him. They circled the camp for half a mile and called to him, but no greenhorn was to be seen. As they were later assembling, Gun Smith happened to hear a noise in the top of the scraggly live oak. There hung the half-crazed Pee-wee, clinging to the topmost branches, scared literally out of his senses.

Gun Smith and the others tried to tell him that there was no further danger, that the terrible Wouser was surely dead, but nothing could persuade him to come down. When they saw that further coaxing was useless, they went back to their pallets and slept soundly for the remainder of the night.

At breakfast the next morning Bean Hole asked casually, "Did you boys have a good night?"

"Why, yes, not a mouse stirred," said Gun Smith, who was eating with real relish. "It's the best night we've had this month." Then looking in the greenhorn's direction, he added with a flickering smile, "Our stranger here is a species of bird all right. . . . It's a regular Pee-wee. It flew the coop while we was all asleep and roosted in the live oak."

Everybody laughed heartily.

Pee-wee, however, was still as pale as a ghost, and could not be coaxed to taste a bite of food.

After breakfast, Gun Smith drew Pee-wee aside and quietly explained that everything had been intended as a joke. He produced the piece of rawhide and showed how he had faked the Lizard. Pee-wee would not believe what was told him until Mushmouth finally gave the blood-curdling howl of the Wouser.

"There's nothin' to be the least ashamed of," Gun Smith assured him. "Just forget it. Everybody comin' to the cattle country for the first time has got it to go through with sooner or later. We was all initiated in our time too, you know."

Gun Smith was so entirely kind that the stranger quickly confided his desire to buy a horse and an outfit and become a real cowboy. "I want the horse that I buy to be the best horse on the whole ranch. He must be able to throw dust in everybody's eyes. You understand what I mean."

"Yes, I understand perfectly," replied Gun Smith quietly, as he realized how much he detested this sort of bragging.

"And will you hire me to work for you?" questioned the stranger with new enthusiasm.

"Why, yes, I'll hire you. . . . We're always in need of more men. Every time Pecos brings home a new herd we have to find outriders to accompany it. We have at least two hundred outriders with our various herds this very minute."

"And do you know where I can get the horse I'm looking for?"

"Let me see, let me see," replied Gun Smith as he tried to think of the horse he would like the greenhorn to buy. "I have it," he added the next minute, "you walk back to town and find Sport McKaye. Tell him Gun Smith sent you. Then offer him one hundred dollars for the broncho he calls Baldy. You'll know the pony by the narrow white stripe between his eyes and by the white stockin' on his right front pastern and the one not quite so high on his left hind foot.

"After that, go to the general store. Tell the proprietor you want the brightest pair of red blankets he's got in stock. Be sure to buy yourself two pearl-mounted Mexican guns and two pearl-handled bowie knives to match them. Get yourself a plaited quirt and a rawhide rope. Buy a Mexican saddle and everythin' else you think you need to go along with it, and then come back and I'll teach you to be a real cowboy in less'n no time at all."

Mr. Pee-wee, as he had come to be called by everyone, lost no time in getting started to town. It was a long trail of five miles and Gun Smith smiled dryly to see him depart so proudly.

When Pee-wee reached town he paid Sport McKaye one hundred dollars for Baldy, the worst little stove-up pack pony in the entire range country. Really, the pony wasn't worth two dollars and a half. At the store he fitted himself out with all the showy things he could lay his hands on. He paid three hundred dollars for everything, when a knowing buyer could have bought the entire layout for less than seventy-five.

When Pee-wee rode back to the ranch he little suspected that he had been cheated out of his very eye teeth. He was, in fact, as happy as a lark.

"Say, but you're a dandy," smiled Gun Smith in greeting. "Why, you look as if you'd just jumped out of the pages of one of these yellow-backed story books," he added in subtle irony, which luckily went entirely over Pee-wee's head.

At supper all the boys pretended to want to trade ponies with Pee-wee. "How much'll you take to boot?" bantered Moon Hennessey, who had one of the best ponies on the ranch. "My horse has got a spavin and a ringbone, he's sprung and he's stringhalted, but aside from a few triflin' blemishes, such as these, I'll warrant him sound as a dollar."

"I wouldn't trade Baldy off at any price," bragged Pee-wee, feeling mighty proud. "Baldy's just the kind of horse I've always dreamed of ownin' some day and you can bet I'm goin' to keep him."

After the boys had exhausted their wits in trying to trade

Pee-wee out of his worthless Baldy, they turned their attention to another topic. Chuck suggested casually that it was about time for the gang to ride in and shoot up Wichita Falls, the nearest trading post.

"This is a little job we do regularly at least once a year, merely as a matter of form," explained Gun Smith, "and I shouldn't be surprised but you're about right."

"Tonight's the only free night I have this week," explained Chuck.

"Me, too," chimed in Moon Hennessey.

"Same here," added Mushmouth.

"All in favor of doin' it tonight, stick up your hands," smiled Gun Smith.

Every hand went up except Pee-wee's.

"What do you say to goin' out on this jaunt with us, Mr. Pee-wee?" asked Gun Smith.

"I'm game for anything, of course, now that I have a horse and outfit!"

"That's a fine spirit," chirped Gun Smith as he slapped the greenhorn across the shoulder hard enough to leave a blister. "Our Boss, Pecos Bill, when he gets back tomorrow and finds you here, will be prouder'n ever of his I. X. L. Outfit. If you make good tonight, he'll likely enough be in favor of promotin' you to the position of Boss of one of his other ranches."

Before time to start on the expedition to paint Wichita Falls red, Gun Smith drew Pee-wee aside and explained carefully just what was to be done. Pee-wee was to ride Baldy up and down the street, shoot first one pearl-handled gun into the air and then the other. He was to give the wildest of war-whoops and pretend he was a regular Indian. If the Sheriff dared show his face, Pee-wee was to call him a runt maverick, put spurs to Baldy and ride away on the wings of the wind.

"If necessary, we'll all be on hand to pull you out. When the Sheriff sees you, he'll run for his life," Gun Smith declared glibly.

The boys kept passing the bottle of red pepper moonshine to Pee-wee before time to start. And he took a hearty nip each time just to prove he was a regular cowhand. So by the time he rode into Wichita Falls, Pee-wee was feeling sure that he could, if it were at all necessary shoot up the Sheriff himself— the runt maverick.

Pee-wee began spurring his stove-up pack pony up and down the only street in town, shooting his revolvers and yelling: "Ee-Yow! Ee-Yow! Ee-Yow!"

The cowboys knew something would happen any minute. So they hid themselves and their ponies in the sage brush nearby.

The Sheriff watched and waited until Pee-wee had completely winded his old nag and had shot his last bullet. He then appeared bravely on the scene. Gun Smith and his men could distinctly hear all that happened. First came the voice of the Sheriff:

"Halt! You're under arrest!"

Immediately afterward sounded the thick voice of Pee-wee. "You're a runt maverick, that's what you are! Get back into your prairie dog hole where you belong!"

There followed then the rapid clatter of hoofs, then a sudden grinding of gravel as the Sheriff grabbed Baldy's rein and brought him to a quick slithering halt. A brief moment of silence followed, and then Pee-wee's thick gutteral: "You're a runt mav—"

At this instant there sang out a quick dull thud as the butt of the Sheriff's quirt came down squarely across Pee-wee's mouth. The end had thus arrived as far as Pee-wee was concerned.

One by one the cowboys sneaked quietly back to the ranch. Gun Smith alone remained behind, and after an hour of waiting he galloped easily into town and stopped casually at the general store.

"Got them buckskin gauntlet gloves in yet?" he asked innocently.

"No, but we've got one of your fool greenhorn mavericks in the calaboose!" announced the Sheriff from the rear of the store.

"You don't say!" Gun Smith replied, pretending to be much astonished. "What's up?"

"Your outfit can't 'runt maverick' Ol' Sol, I want you all to distinctly understand that!"

"Who is it you've got?" Gun Smith asked quietly.

"The dumb greenhorn that paid Sport McKaye a hundred dollars for his worthless stove-up pack pony, Baldy."

"A hundred dollars! I'm sure surprised!" answered Gun Smith, hiding his feelings.

"Yes, a hundred dollars, and Baldy ain't worth more'n a five spot of any man's honest money."

"I'm sure surprised," repeated Gun Smith. "And to think, only this mornin' this Pee-wee told me, as loud as a brass band, that he knowed it all. He said he'd seen the elephant and talked with the owl."

"He's seein' a lot tonight he's never seen before," cackled the Sheriff.

After everybody had laughed heartily, Gun Smith gained

the consent of the Sheriff to bail Pee-wee out of the calaboose, as they called the local jail.

By the time Gun Smith got him and Baldy back to the ranch, Pee-wee was all in. His front teeth were so loose they rattled when he tried to talk and his lips were so swollen and bleeding he could scarcely open his mouth.

Without a word Gun Smith unsaddled Baldy, and told the greenhorn to go to sleep.

Next morning when Pee-wee awoke, he found himself alone. He thought he had gone to sleep with his head on his saddle, but now his head was resting heavily on a stone. He looked here and there and everywhere, but could find nothing.

All this while the cowboys were watching his actions from an ambush. They were so full of laughter that their sides ached.

Finally the greenhorn stamped the very dust of the ranch from his shoes. He hit the trail and began to cut the dirt for town. He was a sadder but wiser man. The elephant had given him a brisk slap with its trunk and the owl was hooting all sorts of wisdom in his ears.

When Pee-wee arrived in town he found Baldy hitched se-curely in front of the general store where he couldn't help but see him. The gaudy red blankets fairly shouted at him and his belt with his brace of empty pistols was hanging limp from his saddlehorn.

Half an hour later, in a bare room, with a rude table and a half dozen rude chairs, Pee-wee found himself facing the stern-looking Judge.

The Judge and the Sheriff both knew that Gun Smith and his crowd were really to blame for all that had happened. They also knew that these cowboys were entirely too clever to allow themselves to become entangled within the meshes of the law.

"Young man," the Judge began slowly, after he had squinted his eyes and cocked his wise old head slightly, "you drink more squirrel whiskey than you can carry. You come into town like a roaring Wouser. You ride up and down the street shooting off your guns as if you thought you were the leader of the Devil's Cavalry. You yell like a wild Indian. You call our much respected Sheriff a runt maverick! You show your utter disrespect for all law and order. Is this a correct statement of your offense?"

"I guess you're right, Judge," Pee-wee answered from the depth of his despair.

"Now, I don't care a continental who your ancestors are nor where you hail from. What I do know is that you've acted like a regular greenhorn. Your first trip in, you buy from Sport McKaye a stove-up pack pony named Baldy for one hundred dollars. Well, sir, that pony ain't worth five dollars of any man's honest money. Next you go to the store and blow in a lot of cash for a no-good, showy outfit. Your second trip in you try to set your heel on our sacred law and order. The only reasonable explanation is that you're a dyed-in-the-wool greenhorn, that you don't realize the kind of law-abiding country you are now in. You're in the greatest country and the best little town God ever made! Remember that!

"The usual fine for your offense is $150.00. The usual sentence is six months in the calaboose on black bread and cold water.

"This is, however, like as not your first offense. You are clearly new to our part of the world. I will remit this sentence and fine under this one condition: You go back out to

I. X. L. ranch and get Pecos Bill to vouch for your conduct."

After the Judge had finished with Pee-wee, Old Sol, the Sheriff, gave him a million dollars' worth of good advice in less than thirty seconds: "If a man knows any secrets about himself, he should die and let them be buried with him, as somebody says somewhere. Remember, my lad, that the man who toots his own horn all the while never finds anybody else to toot for him. The big game to play, lad, is to let the other fellow do all the tooting."

The Sheriff took Pee-wee to see Sport McKaye, and he was glad to return the one hundred dollars. He took Pee-wee to the general store and there the outfit was exchanged for the best that money could buy.

When Pee-wee explained later in the day all that had happened to him, Gun Smith smiled wistfully:

"It's all in the day's work, my lad. The future is kind to the man who forgets today what a fool he made of himself yesterday. I mean, the man who don't allow yesterday to stand in the way of today and tomorrow. We boys just naturally had to have our little fun, you might say. Now that you're initiated, you can get to be a regular cowboy. It's up to you. Want to try?"

"I sure do," Pee-wee answered humbly.

"Well, then, consider yourself hired till Pecos gets home, anyway. Report to Chuck and tell him that I said to give you an honest job."

Pee-wee did as he was told and in time became one of the most skillful with the rope and one of the quietest with his tongue of all the boys in the I. X. L.

XIV.

PECOS BILL BUSTS THE CYCLONE

Gun Smith and his cowmen were so busy with work and play that they did not notice the passing of summer. With the coming of early fall a drouth set in. For weeks the baking sun parched the prairie. The streams dried up and the grass withered to a sere yellow. Day after day the men lived in dust. There was grimy dirt and gritty sand in their hair and eyes and ears. The herded cattle lolled their tongues and grew haggard and fretful.

Pecos Bill finally found it necessary to furnish water for his famishing herds. For a long time he puzzled his brain trying to invent some method that would make him a water boy to all his countless cattle. One day, as a last resort, he lassoed a grove of prickly pear trees and gave Widow Maker the word to go. For hours together he dragged this thorny bundle back and forth at the end of his lariat. Widow Maker flew at breakneck speed and the earth rumbled and the dust rose up until the sky was a dirty gray. By the time Pecos was through with this little chore, he had gouged out a canal ten feet deep and twenty-five miles in length.

Pecos was entirely happy, for he fully expected to awaken next morning and find his canal full of water; but the ground was so thoroughly dried out that no water seeped through. Pecos was thus reduced to another necessity. After thinking things over for another day or two, he decided to try lassoing an oxbow of the Rio Grande River, which was three miles long. He did this easily, lashed his lariat across his saddle-horn, and then set Widow Maker off on the jump. There was a rush and a swish and a sharp tug at his rope, and when he reached the head of his improvised canal he looked back. To his delight he found the big ditch brimming with water.

But by the time the cattle had taken their fill and the water had finished seeping into the dry ground, there was no water left. It thus became necessary for Pecos Bill to lasso ten miles of river each morning. Being naturally a modest man, he did this little job while his cowboys were at their breakfast. They would hear a sudden clatter and roar that sounded as if all the water in the Atlantic Ocean was again coming down at a single bound. Without warning, there would follow a quick grinding of hoofs and out of the cloud of dust Pecos and

Widow Maker would appear before them, quivering as if they had just ended a race for their lives.

"It would be worth a whole year's wages," said Gun Smith, full of wonder, "if only we could get our eyes set quick enough to see Pecos Bill drag up the Rio Grande into the canal."

"It don't seem accordin' to reason," added Chuck loyally, "but I know for a fact that he does lasso the river every single mornin'!"

This was all well and good. But at the end of two months, despite Pecos Bill's fine efforts as water boy, the drouth had become still more terrifying. The prairie grass was as dry as powder and the sage brush as brittle as match wood.

"We'll be deuced lucky if we get out of this without a ragin' prairie fire," the men observed among themselves day after day.

"There'll be some fried gents around here, if ever things get started," said Gun Smith with a flickering smile.

One morning, a week later, the men noticed that the horizon seemed blurred with a gray haze. During the day this haze gradually thickened. Once or twice the men thought they smelled the faint odor of burning grass. The cattle constantly sniffed and bellowed. The men noticed this, too. By good fortune, there was but a slight breeze.

"If an old-fashioned sou'wester should set in today, they'd be some of us hittin' the long trail for Kingdom Come," commented Moon Hennessey, gloomily.

It was early in the forenoon of the following day that the southwester did arrive. The smoke along the horizon rapidly thickened until the sun was entirely blotted out of the sky. Bits of fine gray ash slowly filtered to the ground in grim warning.

Pecos Bill had ridden out on Widow Maker at a perilous gallop to see if there was danger, and now he came dashing back at top speed. He shouted briefly:

"Our one chance to save the herd and ourselves is to start a backfire."

Scarcely had he finished speaking when every man rushed to the work. The outriders circled the terrified cattle and held them from a panic and a stampede. Bundles of faggots were fastened at the end of a lariat. The faggots were lighted and Gun Smith dragged them slowly forward. As the fire parted, two of the other men on their ponies straddled the oncoming blaze and dragged a wet cowhide at the tail of their lariats to smother the flame. The other men followed at close range and beat out any remaining sparks with switches made from bundles of twigs.

The backfire, thus left to take its course, ran forward into the teeth of the wind and offered protection against the oncoming big prairie blaze.

All day long the men labored at the perilous task and by the time the prairie fire arrived they had cut themselves and their herd off by several square miles of burned-over ground.

"Say, do you know," smiled Gun Smith when they had come back to the ranch shack for food and water, "we look worse'n a bunch of singed tomcats!"

It was only too true. Here reclined Chuck and Pee-wee and Moon Hennessey and all the rest, with charred eyebrows and blistered faces and sooty, smarting hands. But they were happy, for they had saved their own lives as well as their herd.

The men slept like knots in a log that night and next morning got up expecting to pass a quiet day. They should have known that a spurt of hard luck chases right on the heels of another. The prairie fire was over. But something else worse was coming.

During the morning the sky was still a dull gray from the smoke, but by noon it lowered with a more ominous black. By early afternoon the wind had died down until there was not even the faintest breeze. The air suddenly grew heavy and oppressive and the heat became unbearable. A tremendous, awesome silence fell over all things. The cattle drowsed and loitered listlessly.

After a time the herd suddenly changed its mood and became touchy and nervous. The cattle sniffed the heavy air and snorted and bellowed and threatened to break into a stampede. All this while the sky was becoming more and more inky.

"We're in for a cyclone!" called Gun Smith with drawn face. "Come on, boys. Throw as many of the cattle as we can into some sort of shelter."

"Let's divide the herd and keep them from stampeding, if possible," Pecos Bill answered hurriedly.

As he spoke, Pecos leapt astride of Widow Maker and the next moment was riding among the bewitched cattle, talking to them in their own language and starting them slowly in various directions. The other men followed at his heels and together they soon had the cattle moving, thus diverting their attention from the coming storm.

As the men looked, they noted that the blackness was becoming shaded a deep greenish copper. From out the blackness boomed a sullen crash of thunder.

The men now showed neither horse nor cattle mercy. They quirted and spurred and threatened every bolting steer with wild yelling.

In another instant the men heard a long-drawn purring moan, then a series of quick snapping reports of thunder.

"She loves me . . . She loves me not . . . She loves me . . . She loves me not . . . She loves me . . ." Gun Smith crooned, as if tearing petals from a daisy, as each flash of lightning struck nearer and nearer in rapid succession.

"Be careful there! Raise your sights, God!" shouted Moon Hennessey. "You sure got me dancin'! Say, can't you find a better mark'n me for your greased lightnin'?"

"Hell's broke loose!" shrieked Mushmouth. "And now the Devil's to pay!"

Soon there was a threatening roar, then a lightning-fringed black funnel moved menacingly out of the depths of the greenish-copper darkness. As the men noted the direction in which the funnel was moving, they turned their cattle as best they could to the right of where its central swirl would come.

And now between the crashes of the thunder the men heard a wild "Ee-Yow! Ee-Yow!" They looked, and what did they see but Pecos Bill riding Widow Maker swiftly out to meet the oncoming hurricane.

They couldn't believe their eyes. Even Pecos Bill had never done anything like that before. Not a man of them but felt Pecos had met his match this time. "Stop!" yelled Gun Smith.

But Pecos Bill went right on. As he neared the menacing funnel he unfurled his agile lariat, whirled its spreading loop about his head and hurled it in defiance at the head of the approaching monster.

"Pecos Bill's ropin' the cyclone!" now shouted Gun Smith breathlessly.

The next moment the men saw Pecos leap headlong into the air and disappear amid the blackness. Widow Maker,

Pecos Bill hurled his lariat at the head of the approaching monster

finding himself free, dashed to one side just in time to avoid being carried into the swirling monster's maw. He lost the tip of his tail in the wind at that, but he was lucky to get off with his life.

With a whizz and a deafening roar and a bang, the cyclone leapt directly over their heads and was gone. After they had rounded up their crazed cattle, they rode back and forth along the path of the storm to see if they could find any remains of Pecos Bill. They felt sure he had been thrown before he could really get on top of the funnel. And if by any chance he was still alive, they wanted to ease his pain as best they could.

"Look at the tracks the cyclone left," said Gun Smith as they went along. "It reared off the earth when Pecos Bill got his noose around its neck. And look at the way it kicked. Talk about *skyscrapin'* and *high flyin'*. This cyclone critter jumped more than three miles the first shot!"

"Sure did, and it's plain enough," added Chuck loyally, "we have Pecos to thank for our not bein' blown entirely off the planet! If the old buckaroo hadn't jumped just when he did, we'd have been lifted clean out of Kingdom Come!"

"I tell you, there never was a rider like Pecos Bill," added Gun Smith in awe. "Nobody else that lived anywhere could hold a candle to him. Scared mavericks—that's what anybody else'd been if they'd met up with an honest-to-goodness Texas twister. They'd have run for their lives the same as we done."

"Shut your face!" snarled Moon Hennessey. "You've seen the last you're ever goin' to of your sweet son of a Coyote! Pecos has tried his high jinks once too often! He needn't think he can sit there in the sky, floppin' his hat across the ears of the moon!"

"Far as we know, the old buckaroo ain't made Pecos eat his

dust yet!" answered Gun Smith. "We've been up and down the old vinegaroon's trail a dozen times and the most we've been able to discover is an old camp kettle turned wrong side out. I'm tellin' you anybody that can ride Widow Maker can ride anythin'!"

"You talk like a locoed longhorn steer looks!" cut in Moon Hennessey. "Anythin' that can turn a cast-iron kettle inside out can't be handled."

"Since you're so certain," answered Gun Smith hotly, "I'll just bet you three months' wages that Pecos Bill'll succeed in bustin' the cyclone, funnel and all."

"Now that I'm talkin' to a business man, I'll just make it a bet of six months' salary!" barked Moon Hennessey. "You fellows have been makin' a hero out of this triflin' greenhorn once too often, as you'll soon find out."

"If it wasn't for losin' this perfectly good bet," answered Gun Smith, "I'd up and knock you into the middle of next February for your unkind remarks! You better be mighty careful or there'll be war!"

All this time that the cowboys were arguing Pecos Bill was having the ride of his life. "Multiply Widow Maker by a thousand or a million," he was singing to himself as he whirled about like a Dervish of the desert.

Before he had leapt from the back of Widow Maker he had clutched his bowie knife between his teeth and a twenty-dollar gold piece in his hand. "Anywhere I land, if I'm alive, I can get on if I keep these," he had thought to himself.

Down across Texas the cyclone tore, *cake-walking* and *twisting* and *sun-fishing* worse than a whole herd of outlaw bucking bronchos.

When the old twister found that it could not free itself of

Pecos Bill by shaking him off its back, it tried to scare him to death. It reached down and pulled up a half dozen mountains by the roots and threw them at Pecos' head. The trouble with all this was that Pecos dodged so fast that the cyclone couldn't see where he was half of the time.

When the cyclone saw that mountains were too large and two clumsy to handle, it was madder than ever and went racing down across New Mexico. In fact, it was so perfectly furious it tore up every tree that crossed its path and cracked them like a thousand rawhide quirts. This was a lot more dangerous than a few loose mountains, and Pecos Bill knew it. His body was being severely bruised, his clothes torn into shreds. So terrible was the cyclone's rage that it left the whole section of the country it crossed entirely bare. Later on people had to set stakes to find their way across it. This is the way the Staked Plains, as they are still known, came about.

All this made Pecos Bill mighty unhappy. But he hung right on and never said a word. And pretty soon the old cyclone began to get the idea.

Why, Pecos was actually rolling a cigarette and lighting it from a flash of lightning!

This made the cyclone so furious it didn't know where it was going. It raced across Arizona. It dug in its toes as it went and tore a gulley through the heart of the mountains. This put Pecos Bill in a worse fix than ever. He not only had to dodge the original mountains the cyclone had picked up and the thousands of trees swirling in every direction, but now the air was becoming so full of dust and pieces of rock that he had to blow with all his might before he could take a full breath.

His only safety lay in his dodging so fast that the cyclone

couldn't get its eyes on him. If it ever had found out where
he really was, for a minute, it would have buried him under a
mighty pile of earth and rocks.

Pecos was just beginning to think he couldn't last much
longer when the cyclone came to the same conclusion. A
busted broncho couldn't have felt worse. And no matter what
the cyclone did, it just naturally couldn't get rid of Pecos Bill.

Just then, however, it had another bright idea. It would
rain out from under him! Now as soon as Pecos saw what
was happening he said to himself: "This is the same tactics a
broncho uses when he rears over on his back. The only thing
left for me to do now is to jump."

The water beneath him was falling in torrents and regular
waterspouts. So fast was the downfall that the water rushed
through the great gully that the cyclone had just cut between
the mountains, and quick as a wink made the Grand Canyon of the Colorado.

Pecos Bill began to look hard in every direction to see where
he'd better jump. If the sky beyond the edge of the cyclone
hadn't been clear, he wouldn't have known in the least where
he was, for by this time he was a thousand feet above the
limit of the very highest clouds.

Beneath him lay huge piles of jagged rock and he couldn't
help remembering how Old Satan looked after he had been
dragged down from the top of Pike's Peak. So he turned his
eyes in other directions. Pecos did not for a minute doubt
his own ability to grow a complete new skeleton if he had to.
But he didn't want to waste more time than was necessary
getting back to the ranch. And a new skeleton did take time.

Looking out at the horizon in every direction, he saw in
the southwest what looked to be a soft cushion of sand. Quickly

setting his foot on a passing crest of mountain, he kicked himself off into space with a gigantic bound.

For what seemed an incredible time he flew through the empty air. He was so terribly high that, for the first half hour, he was afraid he might be flying right off the earth. So he began looking around to see if the moon was anywhere in his immediate vicinity.

Then gradually he saw beneath him what looked like a sea of golden haze reaching up its hands to catch him. Slowly the haze cleared and the golden glow became very dazzling. Soon it was wildly leaping, right up toward him, and the next instant there was a terrible crash. Pecos Bill thought his ears had exploded and that his legs were completely telescoped inside his body. Sand had splashed on all sides like a wave of the sea.

When he finally came to his senses he saw he was in the bottom of what seemed an enormous shallow bowl. Sand, sand, sand—farther than he could see in every direction.

Pecos Bill slowly got up on his feet. His entire body was as sore as a boil and he couldn't muster the courage to touch himself to see if his bones were still inside him or not. When he found that he could still walk he felt better. "Guess I won't need a new skeleton this trip," he grinned.

The fact was that in falling he had splashed out the greatest depression in the Southwest. And down at the bottom he had left the impression of his hip pockets in bed rock. In short, he had just made Death Valley, which can be seen to this day, bed rock and all.

"If only Slue-foot Sue could have been along," Pecos sighed, forlorn lover that he was. "She'd have enjoyed every minute."

Then he remembered something else and opened his hand.

At first he couldn't quite believe his eyes. The cyclone had blown his twenty-dollar gold piece into two half dollars and a plugged nickel.

Quickly he took the bowie knife from between his teeth. Here was another jolt. The wind had blown it into a dainty pearl-handled penknife.

"I seem to be in the middle of nowhere," sighed Pecos. "What can I do without money and without a real knife?"

Then a smile overspread his face: "Ready made presents, I'll say. The plugged nickel I'll give to Gun Smith, and the pearl-handled knife—to Slue-foot Sue, with my love."

But where was the ranch? Which way should he go to get back to the boys? Pecos couldn't make out in the least. For a minute he was more unhappy than he had ever been in his life. Then he suddenly remembered. He'd just call on the Coyotes and in no time at all he'd be hustling along on his way back.

XV.

THE MYSTERIOUS STRANGER

While these things were happening to Pecos Bill the I. X. L. ranch was getting into a terrible snarl. As the days lengthened into weeks and the weeks added themselves into months, Gun Smith and Chuck began to wonder whether, after all, they would ever see Pecos again. But they never said so, and whenever either of them met Moon Hennessey or any of his followers they whistled vigorously to keep up their courage.

"What's the worry?" Gun Smith would say, "Pecos'll be

back any day now. That old Cyclone cayuse most likely ran
a thousand or two miles before he had the sense to admit he
was busted. And it just naturally'll take Pecos several weeks
to find his way home."

"Find his way home—nothin'!" came Moon Hennessey's
reply. "You've seen the last you'll ever see of that cayuse!"

"If it wasn't for losin' the money I've bet you on his return,
I'd make you take that name back or eat dust!" Gun Smith
growled.

"Oh, yes? And speakin' of the bet, how about payin' up
right now, not to mention dividin' up? We've got enough
steers now to make everybody a millionaire. Pay up, divide
up, and shut up, I say."

"Keep your shirt on, Moon. What's the idea of gettin'
galled under the saddle?"

"I've been a cucumber long enough, I'm tellin' you!"

"All you've been is a bitin' red pepper ever since Pecos Bill
stepped aboard the hurricane deck of that old twistin' buckaroo!"

"All right. And that's just what I'm goin' to keep on bein' until you use a little horse sense," concluded Moon.

Hour after hour and day after day the quarrel kept up.
Not content with waiting peaceably, Moon Hennessey and his
faction now began to plan open rebellion.

"We'll shoot Gun Smith and Chuck and their flunkies the
same as if they was varmint porcupines or skunks," bragged
Moon secretly to his friends.

After another week of waiting, Gun Smith and Chuck were
at their wits' end. They knew what Moon and his crowd were
up to and they never took their hands off their guns, not even
when they went to sleep.

The next thing that happened was that Moon Hennessey had begun to brag that if ever again he laid eyes on Pecos Bill it would be a mighty sorry day for that low-down windbag. He even became so reckless that he began to say so right out in front of Gun Smith and Chuck.

One day when Moon rode down to Wichita Falls he took one too many nips of squirrel whiskey and began to speak his mind.

"Say! If that big bag of wind, Pecos Bill, ever gets back, tell him for me I'm lookin' for him. I'll fill him fuller of lead than a Porcupine has quills!"

"You're gettin' good, ain't you, Moon?" commented Old Sol, the sheriff, quietly.

"Well, if you're around when I happen to meet him, you'll soon see," Moon bragged. "That son of a Coyote has got himself bragged up around these parts until he's got everybody licked. And Gun Smith and Chuck and the rest of 'em join right in on the chorus. Their backbones ain't nothin' but lariats by now. They're so limp bowin' down to him. But I'm goin' to show him. I'll teach him his place. And then we're goin' to divide up the cattle and retire rich. That's what the I. X. L.'s goin' to do."

Now while Moon Hennessey was doing this bragging a quiet stranger was leaning across one of the counters toward the rear of the store. He had on a Christy-stiff hat pulled down low over his eyes, a boiled shirt and a stand-up collar. He now sauntered carelessly up to Moon, held out his hand and said:

"Mister, I like your line of talk. You sound like a real cowman. If you are the Boss out at this I. X. L. ranch you've been sayin' so much about, I'd like to strike you for a job."

Moon Hennessey looked hard at the newcomer. The features seemed to resemble someone that Moon had seen, but who he was Moon couldn't make out. If Moon had thought to look, he would have noticed that the stranger had uncommonly large feet. He would have seen, too, that the stranger was wearing a black wig to conceal red hair. As it was, Moon thought the stranger a greenhorn dude.

"Well, I'm not exactly the Boss, but I'm goin' to be any day now. So I guess you won't have any trouble landin' something."

Moon Hennessey was always looking for recruits and this stranger seemed to offer very possible material for another loyal member of his gang.

"Where you punched cows?" asked Moon curiously.

"Over in Missouri. We had about a dozen cows, me and my pa, I guess."

When the stranger said Missouri, Moon smiled. No Texas cowboy ever admitted that a Missourian was anything but a greenhorn and a tenderfoot. A dozen cows made Moon smile still more. Another chance for an initiation! Moon now urged the stranger by all means to come along out to the ranch.

It happened to be about an hour before dinner when Moon Hennessey and the cowman from Missouri arrived at the ranch house. Bean Hole was busily getting things ready.

The day was hot and the stranger appeared to be all tuckered out. He took a long drink of water from the spring, then lay down under a large live-oak tree to rest until the meal was ready. The stranger laid aside his Christy-stiff hat and was soon apparently fast asleep.

"Wait till we get through with this greenhorn dude," bragged Moon in a whisper to Bean Hole.

"Better be careful what you say," answered the cook softly. "Some of these strangers sleep with one ear to the breeze."

"Let him get his ear full if he wants. He's in for a good drubbin', whatever happens. Dudes don't set any too well around here, you know, Bean Hole."

Suddenly Gun Smith and his men galloped in from work and when they discovered the stranger and his Christy-stiff hat they stopped abruptly, twenty or thirty feet from where he lay, and began talking loudly for his benefit.

"What do you think we ought to do about it?" asked Gun Smith in a loud tone which he fondly thought was a frightened one.

"We can't do anythin' until we know what it is," responded Chuck.

"It's a Bear or some worse varmint!" added Mushmouth, equally terrified.

"No, it's the dangerous Mountain Lion," corrected Chuck. "Looks as if it was infected with hydrophobia, too!"

"I believe it's one of them poisonous critters that run on two legs up and down the river and screech 'Walo! Wahoo!'" declared Rusty Rogers.

Bean Hole and Moon Hennessey were full of glee. They were off to a good start and as soon as the stranger woke up they'd go right ahead with the program. But the greenhorn did not move a muscle. Had he heard what they were saying? The men couldn't be sure, but it was worth taking a chance on.

"Boys, it's a downright shame for us to stand by and see a good man like this ate up by such a terrible varmint!" Gun Smith yelled with a tone of deepest seriousness. Then suddenly raising his voice, he shouted: "Look out there, stranger, that thing's just ready to leap on you and devour you!"

The stranger did what he knew was expected of him. He leapt up and ran like a scared jackrabbit. And before he had time to turn around, the men had each fired three quick volleys into the Christy-stiff hat.

Then Gun Smith climbed gingerly down from his broncho and picked up a long stick. With his gun ready, he approached the bullet-riddled hat and turned it over slowly. As he put his gun back into its holster he remarked:

"Boys, whatever kind of varmint it is, it's sure dead all right!"

The stranger stopped in his tracks, turned and came fearfully back. When he saw his Christy-stiff hat, he solemnly discussed the averted calamity.

"You boys sure did save me," he said seriously. Then suddenly he burst into laughter. All the boys joined in and promptly invited him to dinner. This greenhorn wasn't so bad, they thought. He could take a joke.

After the meal was finished, the stranger said to Gun Smith: "I heard this mornin' you need a man, so I came out to get the job."

"What kind of a job do you think you're lookin' for?" asked Gun Smith.

"Why, I want to be a cowpuncher," replied the tenderfoot with an innocent baby-eyed stare.

"And what do you know about cowpunchin'?"

"Oh, I know a lot about it."

"Where have you punched cows?"

"Down in Missouri, mister," replied the stranger again, still with the same pop-eyed innocence.

Gun Smith winked at the men and they all smiled to think that this tenderfoot thought he had learned cowpunching in

Missouri. Their notion of a Missourian was that he was so green he'd finally have to be hung up in the sun for a month to dry before Satan could make any headway on him with the sulphur flames.

"And what kind of an outfit did you work for?"

"Well, I don't know as you'd exactly call it an outfit. You see, I worked for my pap. Pap had somewhere nigh onto twenty cows. It was my job to take them down to water mornings and evenings. Sometimes I rode Pap's old gray mare, Katie, and sometimes I rode the donkey, Jake. My ma said I could ride real nice."

Gun Smith was becoming disgusted with such childish prattle. He thought he had seen plenty of tenderfeet before, but this Missourian took the cake.

"I'm sorry," he said crisply, "but I guess we haven't any job here big enough for you."

"What?" wailed the stranger. And it looked to Gun Smith as if he might cry any minute. "You don't mean to say you're not goin' to give me a chance? Maybe you don't think I can ride well enough for your outfit?"

"I guess you've got your rope on exactly the right steer," replied Gun Smith, more disgusted than anything.

"But won't you give me a chance to show you what I can do? Ma always said I was a real good rider."

"W-e-ll," replied Gun Smith, "I guess we could give you a chance, all right. You see the head of that pinto broncho stickin' over the edge of the corral there?"

"Why, yes, I see it."

"That's General Stonewall Jackson. Well, you ride him, and if he doesn't buck you into the middle of Kingdom Come in less than thirteen seconds, I'll give you a job."

"Stonewall Jackson's some name for a horse!" exclaimed the wide-eyed innocent. "You say if I ride old Stonewall Jackson that you'll give me a job right away? That's fine! And would you mind buyin' me an outfit, too? You see, I'm terribly hard up. About all I got is a plugged nickel!"

"Yes, I'll give you a job and throw the outfit in, if that's what you want," said Gun Smith.

"Oh, thank you! Now bring on your horse," the stranger replied as excited as a small boy who is on his way to his first circus.

Old Stonewall Jackson was the worst piece of horse flesh on the entire ranch. He was an outlaw and a man-killer. He was such a terror that all the men were afriad to go near him. Gun Smith was the only man who had ever ridden him, and even Gun Smith had promised himself never to tackle the job again.

It seemed rather a low-down trick to play on the tenderfoot; but he was so green he was just jumping at the chance to give an exhibition of the quickest way to break his fool neck. Besides, the men all thought he would never get near enough to the old General to get hurt.

Finally Gun Smith called out:

"Moon Hennessey, you and Mushmouth catch and saddle old General Stonewall Jackson and bring him here. Our Missouri friend thinks he can ride him."

After a lot of trouble the cowboys succeeded in lassoing the old General. They threw him, blindfolded him so that they could more nearly manage him, then bridled and saddled him. They tied two ropes to his bridle, and Moon Hennessey at a safe distance on one side, and Mushmouth on the other, led General Stonewall in with tight ropes to keep him from charging them. Even with this precaution, he kept them both busy bringing him up to where Gun Smith and the tenderfoot were waiting.

"But you don't expect me to ride on such a queer saddle as that? Why, the saddle me and my pap had wasn't one-tenth as big as that thing! Won't you please, mister, ask them to take it off? I'd much prefer to ride bareback."

Gun Smith was entirely disgusted by this time with the greenhorn's utter stupidity.

After the saddle was taken off with the greatest difficulty the tenderfoot said:

"My pap and me never used any such fancy kind of bridle, either. We always had just a halter. Perhaps, mister, you won't object to askin' them to take off the bridle, too. You see, I think I'll do better if I ride the same way I've been used to do down in Missouri."

The men had a hard time, indeed, in putting on the halter. Old General Stonewall Jackson surely lived up to his worst reputation, rearing and biting, striking with his forefeet and kicking with his heels. He was so vicious it was dangerous to get within half a mile of him.

"That seems a sort of ornery kind of horse you've brought me to ride. I guess I'll have some little trouble in gettin' myself settled squarely on his back. Of course, after I'm on his back, I'll not be afraid. It's principally the gettin' on that's troublin' me now."

"That's what troubles the most of us most of the time," answered Gun Smith with cold sarcasm. "But Chuck here'll give you a leg-up."

"Oh, no, my pap wouldn't want me to let you do that. He used to tell me if I couldn't get on my horse alone, I'd better stick to walkin'. I guess I'll have a try at him, if you fellows are ready."

Moon Hennessey and Mushmouth were more than ready. They had been dodging and jerking until they were worn out. Besides, everybody was bursting to see the fun. It was only a question of how far the greenhorn would fly through the air before he landed. It would do their hearts good to see this dude eat the dust.

Then, without warning, the tenderfoot rushed at old General Stonewall Jackson, buried his hand in the broncho's mane and landed lightly astride. When the old General became conscious of what was happening, his rider was already yelling and slapping his ears with the halter strap.

It was a hundred times better than a circus performance to watch the old General open his bag of tricks. He tried everything he had. He bucked endways, he bucked backwards, he bucked sideways, crossways and every which way. There was such a cloud of dust that the cowboys couldn't see half that was happening.

"We're a crowd of idiots!" exclaimed Gun Smith, finally. "That's no greenhorn! He's an impostor, a cheat! And now I'm in for buyin' him a complete outfit!"

"He's almost as good a rider as Pecos Bill!" shouted Chuck.

As they were watching they saw the stranger let go his hold of the mane, wave his arms carelessly about, and then sing a merry song:

"Sing 'er out, my bold coyotes! leather fists and leather throats,
　　Tell the stars the way we rubbed the haughty down.
We're the fiercest wolves a-prowling and it's just our night for
　　howling,
　　Ee-Yow! a-riding up the rocky trail from town!"

After a long, bitter fight, old General Stonewall Jackson decided he had met his master. Gradually he began to quiet down; and as he did so the stranger began to pat him gently and croon:

> "Whoopee! tu yi yo, git along, little dogies,
>   It's your misfortune and none of my own,
> Whoopee ti yi yo, git along, little dogies,
>   For you know that Texas will be your new home."

Gun Smith scratched his head and his eyes brightened as he commented to Chuck: "He's singin' the same two songs that girl, Slue-foot Sue, sung that day up at Pinnacle Mountain!"

"You're right," answered Chuck. "It's a strange coincidence!"

When old Stonewall Jackson finally decided to stop bucking, the stranger slipped down easily from his back, placed his shoulder under the horse's head and began stroking his cheek and feeding him lumps of sugar. The terrifying old General thus became just an ordinary broncho, eating out of his master's hand.

The next minute the stranger snatched off his wig and stood in his natural person before his bewildered cowpunchers.

"You don't mean to tell me this gentle critter is the worst horse you own!" he smiled. "Why don't you bring on Widow Maker?"

When Gun Smith and the others realized that this was the genuine Pecos Bill they were too astonished for words. They looked down over their noses and couldn't think of a single thing to say.

"Well, how are you, old Gun Smith?" Pecos laughed as he

came forward to shake each man's hand. "And you, Chuck? And you, Moon Hennessey, you, Mushmouth—one and all! But you fellows don't act as if you are exactly glad I've come back."

"Glad ain't quite a strong enough word to use," answered Gun Smith, still feeling very much at a loss to find his tongue. "We're simply delighted!"

As the attention centered on Gun Smith, Moon Hennessey turned on his heels and started as fast as his legs could carry him in the direction of his pony. He had suddenly made up his mind to ride speedily out of the range country.

"Stop your running, Moon, and come straight back here," shouted Pecos Bill.

Moon stopped in his tracks, for he certainly wasn't sure but what some flying lead would follow him. He returned with a hangdog expression.

"Moon," said Pecos tenderly, "remember that you and me are friends, whatever happens. You're going to stay right here on this ranch and go straight on with your work. You're to have the same pay and the same general good treatment that you've always had. Bygones between us shall be bygones. What do you say?"

"After all that happened down at the General Store this mornin', I think I'd better be goin' for good."

"Forget it!" laughed Pecos heartily. "Can't a man be allowed to have his little brag without being held strictly to account? Say, forget it instantly. Give me your hand!"

Moon Hennessey stepped awkwardly forward and Pecos fairly paralyzed his fingers in his hearty grip. As he did so, he added: "Let's turn in and celebrate the death of our terrible old varmint, Mr. Grudge!"

All the men understood what was in Pecos Bill's mind and each man drew his gun and fired a volley into the air. Moon Hennessey's deep-seated enmity was never again mentioned on the range.

That night Moon said wistfully to his nearest friend: "What kind of critter is this Pecos Bill, when outlaw horses like old General Stonewall Jackson eat out of his hand and he's so nice to skunks like me?"

"All I know about it," answered Rusty Rogers, "is that Pecos don't belong to no ordinary breed of buckaroos I happen to be familiar with. He's close to being somethin' like the ninth wonder of the world!"

XVI.

SLUE-FOOT SUE DODGES THE MOON

Of course, Gun Smith and his men were bursting with curiosity to hear all about Pecos Bill's success at busting the cyclone. Gun Smith and Moon Hennessey were, in addition, personally interested because of their bet. But all the while Pecos was slow to talk about his adventure. He did, finally, after the men had plagued him almost to death with their questions, give them a few of the larger details.

"Yes, I believe I succeeded, after a fashion, in busting the old buckaroo; but we made a lot of Geography—the cyclone and I—while I was doing it. If you can imagine the old broncho pulling up mountains by their roots and making a flat empty plain out of a hilly region that had been covered with dense forests; yes, and if you can imagine its scooping out a wonderful Grand Canyon in its wrath, and then not being able to bury me in it, you have some faint notion, perhaps, of the punishment I was put through."

"But how did you get back to earth again?" asked Moon Hennessey, sparring for a chance to win his bet with Gun Smith.

"When the cayuse finally saw he couldn't buck me off or scare me quite to death, nor crush me between whirling rocks, there was only one thing left for him to do. He started to rain out from under me."

"I knew you had busted it!" Gun Smith exploded, feeling that he had already collected his bet.

"Roughly speaking, I must have been up five or six hundred thousand feet in the air, and there were miles and miles of the jagged canyon walls holding up their hands, ready to bury me for all time to come. I was what you call in the middle of a bad fix. I looked in this direction and then in that, until I saw a sandy plateau that I couldn't see the end of. This was my chance. I made a jump into the very center of it. And when I landed several hours later, there was a splash of sand on all sides like a wave at sea after an earthquake."

"And so you consider that you actually busted the old broncho, without a doubt?" Gun Smith exclaimed. "You see, Moon Hennessey and me has a small bet up over your success with the old twister."

"Well, you'll have to settle that little point between yourselves. Of course, when it rained out from under itself and me, there wasn't any broncho of a cyclone left to bust," answered Pecos Bill dreamily.

"But you say you were forced to jump!" urged Moon Hennessey. "And in bustin' a broncho, one of the first and last rules of the game is to stay with the critter till he gives in."

"But—" argued Gun Smith.

In the end Gun Smith and Moon Hennessey had to call off their bet and consider it a draw. The longer they argued, the less they agreed, and soon the entire outfit was about equally divided over the issue. Everybody, however, considered Pecos Bill the champion rider of the Western Hemisphere, if not of the entire Solar System. Even Moon was enthusiastic, especially since he didn't have to pay his six months' wages to Gun Smith.

It was a day or two later that Pecos Bill invited Gun Smith and Moon Hennessey and Chuck and Mushmouth and two or three others to go with him to Pinnacle Mountain.

"I've just come from visiting the place," he had announced.

"What's the old smarty got up his sleeve now?" Moon Hennessey asked joyously.

"I bet it's got something to do with Slue-foot Sue," Gun Smith answered with a broad smile.

"You see," explained Pecos, "my lord's had his troubles. Every other week there's some sort of stampede on the part of the fool steers. Down they go, horns over tails, into the valley. You'd think that steers'd learn something in time, but no. They're just about as idiotic as the human race. It's the same thing over and over, month after month."

"But all this is my lord's business, not ours," urged Gun Smith.

"I grant you that, and besides, my lord is not blaming us for anything, at least not much. You see, I've been at Pinnacle Mountain quite frequently ever since he took the place over. On my way here and there, I've made it a point to stop and see how things are going. And every time I've managed to round up a new herd of steers to restock the ranch. It'd become monotonous to my lord if there should come a time when there weren't any more steers to play cartwheel down into the valley, nor any more corral fence to be mended. Really the prairie-dogs have been wonderful to me on several different occasions. As long as I keep his herd replenished, you see, he hasn't got anything in particular against any of us."

"And how about them short-legged calves? Do they try to pull off a stampede, too?" Gun Smith laughed.

"The one hope of the Perpetual Motion Ranch is in members of the younger generation. They always keep their short-legged side next the mountain, and it makes no difference how often they stampede, they always run in a perfect circle. There's only one fault with these critters: They can't be driven off to market. My lord tried to sell some of them once and it was comical to hear him tell about it. When he drove the poor critters on the level plain they had to run in a circle as fast as they could run in order to keep from falling over on their side.

"As soon as they stopped they went down. A few of them managed to rest a minute by leaning against a tree till they could get their breath, but most of 'em had to be butchered on the spot. My lord looks forward with joy to the day when he can afford to build a packing house and a canning factory at the foot of the mountain. He thinks then he'll have a bonanza at his very door step, for sure."

"And has Slue-foot Sue learned to ride a broncho yet as good as a catfish?" asked Gun Smith with a sharp look at Pecos Bill's face.

Pecos took a few seconds to pull himself together before he attempted to answer.

"Sue's a wonderful broncho buster," he said wistfully. "She takes to a cayuse as naturally as a porcupine quill takes to a broncho's heels. You see, on one of my trips I roped a calico pony and gentled it. Later I took it along up to Pinnacle Mountain and taught her to ride it."

"And has her mother said she could wear cowpuncher pants?" Gun Smith laughed.

"Well, yes and no," Pecos explained. "You see, Gun Smith, the mother and Sue are something like you and Moon. They've got strong minds of their own. Sue was determined to wear chaps like a cowman, and her mother was equally determined that she should wear a skirt. Finally they compromised, which is better than you and Moon have done. And so Sue wears both—one over the top of the other, you understand."

"All dressed up, eh, Pecos?" laughed Gun Smith.

"Yes, but this is only half of it. The mother says Sue's now got to wear one of those big spring-steel bustles the English think're so smart. Which would be all right in its way if the bustle didn't make it ten times harder for Sue to keep in the saddle when her broncho is galloping. Every time the horse strikes the ground the spring in the bustle just naturally throws her up into the air. And she looks like one of those six-weeks-old blackbirds that ain't yet quite got all the tail feathers."

"You told her that, Pecos?" inquired Gun Smith.

"Tell her!" Pecos Bill exclaimed. "Of course I did. Why, we both laughed about it till we almost cried. Finally she said,

Sue wore chaps, skirt, and bustle

'If you had a wife, Pecos, would you force her to wear both skirt and chaps? And would you force her to wear spring-steel bustles when she goes riding?' And I replied, 'If I ever have a wife, she can wear any old thing she wants.' "

"Then what did she say?" Gun Smith asked, hiding his rising excitement.

"Why, if you must know, what she said was, 'How I do wish I were your wife.' 'You mean that?' I asked, drawing in a deep breath, I can tell you. 'But isn't there anything you would refuse me?' she queried growing very serious. 'Absolutely nothing in the world,' I told her and I meant it at the moment. But then I thought I'd better make myself a little clearer, so I explained, 'That is, I'd let you do everything except ride Widow Maker. Once he threw the best rider I knew onto the top of Pike's Peak, and, of course, I don't want anything like that to happen to the one woman I love.'

" 'Of course not,' Sue replied much disappointed. And she sure was pouting when she told me. 'Then you don't think I can ride as well as you. Just wait till I can get this old skirt and this spring-steel bustle off, and I'll show you I can ride, even Widow Maker!'

"I asked her, 'Do you really wish you were my wife?' And she replied, 'I don't know anybody whose wife I'd wish to be half so much.' 'Well then, Sue,' I said, 'Keep right on wishing, and it won't be long.' "

"But you don't mean to tell me that you really mean to marry this girl!" Gun Smith demanded coolly.

"Of course I mean to marry Sue. That's just the reason I'm inviting you and Chuck and Moon and the others along to the wedding, so that you can be my bridesmen or groomsmaids or whatever it is you call them. We've sent back East for a minister, and he's due to arrive at Pinnacle Mountain this morning."

There was, of course, great excitement at the I. X. L. Ranch when it was noised about that Pecos Bill was to wed the vivacious Sue. One minute the cowmen laughed in an uproar; the next minute they were like a nest of hornets. For come to think of it, it was funny—and no joke—at the same time. Pecos Bill married? They couldn't believe it.

When the day arrived, Pecos Bill started with his men in the direction of Pinnacle Mountain. He rode a little ahead, very solemn and quiet, as though lost in dreams. After two or three hours he found he couldn't possibly poke along with the others. He wanted to be with his Sue. "I think I'll ride on ahead," he called suddenly. And before anybody could answer, he had given free rein to Widow Maker, and all that the others could see then was a yellowish cloud of dust.

As Gun Smith and the others followed as fast as their bronchos could carry them, they put their feelings into words.

"What'll we do with a woman at I. X. L. Ranch?"

"There ain't no room for a skirt 'round our outfit!"

"No mistake about that, Pecos Bill is sure loco this time."

"With a woman around, Pecos Bill won't be worth as much as a lop-eared maverick."

"Well, judgin' from past experience, we should give him credit for havin' at least a grain of horse sense."

When Gun Smith and Moon and the others arrived at Pinnacle Mountain they asked the mother if she had seen anything of Pecos Bill.

"Colonel Bill, if you please!" she answered proudly with raised eyebrows. "The Colonel and my daughter are out horseback riding, thank you. Won't you come right along in, and make yourselves comfortable until they return? I'm sorry, but my lord and his Eminence, the Right Reverend Doctor Hull, are walking. They're taking a little constitutional before the ceremony begins, don't you know. You'll have to excuse me for the minute—I'm so sorry—but, you see, I am obliged to superintend the dinner."

"So she's already made a Colonel of our Pecos!" Gun Smith snorted under his breath.

"She couldn't think of havin' her daughter marry anybody less than a Colonel, *don't you know!*" Chuck added in disgust.

"I wonder she hasn't made him a Sir Knight of the Garter, or at very least a General!" Mushmouth continued.

"She's made a strong gesture in that direction. The other royal titles'll follow soon enough," Chuck replied, with an amused smile. "Lucky she didn't get hold of any of the rest of us or hard tellin' what kind of monkeys we'd become!"

After a short while the men could hear voices outside. Slue-foot Sue was saying in a nervous, petulant way: "But after we're married you've just got to let me ride Widow Maker! You simply must, I say! You must! You must!"

"But, Sue dear," Colonel Pecos Bill replied with quiet firmness, "you wouldn't thank me if I let you break your neck on the spot, would you?"

"Oh! It's the same old story I've been hearing all my life, wherever I turn! It's can't! Can't! Can't, all the while! But I want you to know that I *will* ride Widow Maker! I say I will! I will!! I will!!! I'll show you that I can ride your old broncho as well as you or any other cowman! I'm no longer a baby, remember that!"

"But, Sue dear," Colonel Bill answered with quiet patience, "don't worry any more about it. There, now, that's the way

I like you to smile. We'll see about it after the wedding."

"Right you are," laughed the girlish voice. "We shall see! We shall see!" she ended, believing she had won her victory.

When Pecos and Sue entered, the men got to their feet stiffly with hats in hand. "Well, when did you arrive?" Pecos began. "Sue, here are my friends . . . This is Gun Smith, this, my brother Chuck, and this, Moon Hennessey."

Sue gave each of the men a warm greeting. "It is just perfectly lovely of you to come so far to witness this important event. The Colonel and I surely do appreciate it. By the way, who is going to be the best man?"

"I rather believe," exclaimed Gun Smith, "that I'd prefer, if it makes no difference to you, to act in the capacity of a groomsmaid or a bridesman, as you might say."

"How wonderful of you!" Sue laughed heartily. "You have put it quaintly, indeed."

All the others joined in the joyous spirit of the occasion, and soon everybody was entirely at ease and happy.

When Slue-foot Sue and Colonel Bill appeared later for the wedding ceremony, the bride was dressed in a dazzling white satin gown. The wide skirt draped itself in flowing, lacy lines over the wide-spreading hoops; the train extended half across the room; and the steel-spring bustle looked very smart indeed! But dearest of all was the sweet face of the bride herself.

The Right Reverend Doctor Hull was quite charmed with the bride. "My lord," he whispered, "I've not seen Sue's equal in years—not in many years!"

Colonel Bill himself had given no little attention to his clothes. He had, in fact, ridden at least two thousand miles to collect the very best of everything that was to be had. His high-heeled boots, with fancy hand stitching, were polished till they shone like a pair of mirrors. His spurs were of solid gold. He was carrying an imported hat he had ridden seven hundred miles to purchase. Its band was of the best Mexican bead work. He had a pair of breeches he had purchased in California. They were a sort of lavender with inch-square checks. His shirt was of white silk and his vest of red satin that was intended by its creator to set every woman's eyes aflame. His coat was covered with delicate Mexican bead work, too.

It was little wonder he was so proud of himself that he carried his head cocked decidedly over his left shoulder. He was so entirely happy that the corners of his mouth almost touched the tops of his ears. In fact, there wasn't a thing to criticise in Pecos Bill's clothes. He was gotten together exactly right for the occasion.

Just before the couple stood in place for the ceremony the Right Reverend gentleman whispered to my lord: "It seems the least bit weird, even though it is deucedly picturesque, to see the bridegroom dressed so entirely out of accord with His Majesty's London costumer's latest togs."

"Oh, I don't mind, since the Colonel is every inch a man, don't you know," my lord smiled in reply. "I rather approve of his costume."

All the boys were feeling very gay and hardly able to wait for things to start. Mushmouth had brought along his lip-piano to play the wedding march. Bullfrog Doyle was fidgeting about, all set to accompany him by dancing a different tune with each foot. Everyone was bursting with fun. That is, all except Sue's mother, who turned so cold that her stare froze on her face like an Egyptian mummy.

And Slue-foot Sue had an even greater shock in store for her mother. For just before the ceremony was about to begin, she gave a whoop and rushed from the room. A moment later she returned, arrayed in sombrero, woolen shirt, chaps, high-heeled boots, jingling spurs and flaming red breeches. "Ee-Yow!" she called. "A cowboy bride for the greatest cowboy in the world," and swung her hat about her head.

Everyone was completely fascinated by the daring of the beautiful woman. It was evident, judging by the brief moment that she took to make the change, that she must have worn the cowboy clothes under her wedding gown.

In her excitement one thing was wrong, however. She had forgotten that she was still wearing her steel-spring bustle. She had it on now, and although everyone knew at once that a bustle wasn't the thing to wear with chaps and spurs, nobody dared make a suggestion that would spoil the girlish bride's feeling of freedom and happiness.

When her mother saw Sue she fairly choked with annoyance. She tried to speak, but the words stuck in her throat. And Sue, seeing her mother speechless, leapt out of the room with another explosive "Ee-Yow!" This action proved quite too much for the mother's highly excited nerves and she threw up her hands and fainted in a heap on the floor. Colonel Bill flew to help the good woman like the chivalrous gentleman that he was.

This was just the chance Sue was looking for. Quick as a flash she ran pell-mell to where Widow Maker was tied and released him. The faithful horse saw her coming and let out a terrific whinny of distress. Colonel Bill instantly understood what Widow Maker meant and almost dropped the mother on the floor in his haste to rescue his bride.

But, alas! Pecos was a fraction of a second too late. He and the others reached the door just in time to see Slue-foot Sue flying upward through the air out of a cloud of dust.

The poor girl, in fact, had been bucked so high that she had to duck her head to let the moon go by. Pecos stood wringing his hands and looking wildly in the direction of his vanishing bride. After an hour and a half of intense anguish on his part, Sue fell back to earth with the speed of a meteor. She struck exactly in the middle of the spring-steel bustle and rebounded like a rocket, and again the sky completely swallowed her up.

Colonel Bill had often found himself in the middle of many a bad fix; but this was the first time in his life he had ever had to admit that he was absolutely helpless and beaten from the start.

When the mother finally revived and discovered she was entirely deserted, she trotted out on the steps to see what could be happening that was of so much more interest than herself. When she saw Sue again fall like a thunderstone and rebound like a cannon ball, she tried to speak, but instead she again fainted dead away. His Eminence happened to discover her a little while later and beckoned to the astonished Gun Smith and Moon Hennessey to carry her into the house.

Chuck and Mushmouth and the others were so excited by the sudden disaster they couldn't think of a thing to do except to stand open-mouthed and watch for the next return trip of Sue. Back she came, only to go up again. After three or four hours of this suspense, Gun Smith had a bright idea. He found his way over to where the Colonel was pacing back and forth with clenched fists, watching in the general direction whence the bride had last flown, and said:

"Pecos, why in the name of creation don't you lasso her next time she comes flyin' down?"

"I had already thought of that," replied Pecos from the depth of an ocean of despair, "but I'm afraid the rope would cut her in two. Just think of the terrific speed she's traveling!"

"But can't you catch her in your arms or somethin'?" Gun Smith continued hopefully.

"I might, if it wasn't for that confounded steel-spring bustle; but with that on, I'm sure it would kill us both!"

After ten or a dozen of these lightning-like bounces, Sue began to realize her novel situation. Once, as she came whizzing past, she succeeded in timing her shrieks just right, so that her Colonel heard:

"S-t-o-p m-e!"

When Pecos was entirely unable to do this Sue tried to shout other of her wishes; but her words sounded only like a siren as she flew whizzing away into the sky.

After a prolonged conference with His Eminence, my lord walked over to where the Colonel was waiting and said emphatically: "I say, Colonel, why don't you stop her?"

"Why don't you stop her yourself?" retorted Pecos.

"But, don't you know, I didn't start her!"

"And neither did I!" replied Pecos. "The fact is, I did everything possible to prevent the calamity. But you know Sue!"

"But, how shall I say, it's surely your fault. You tempted her with your bucking broncho!"

"I didn't tempt her, I'm telling you. The very name of the horse should have been a warning," Pecos replied, out of patience. "I told her it was risky to ride Widow Maker!"

Slue-Foot Sue bounces on her bustle

"Evidently you know very little about women," my lord declared. "When you said your horse was dangerous, it was the best way to make her want to ride him. That's women for you."

Despite their argument, Slue-foot Sue kept right on bouncing up and down. During the second day Pecos began to collect his wits and throw strings of dried beef around Sue's neck to keep her from starving to death. By timing his arm perfectly with her rebound, he was able to thus lasso food around her neck nearly every time he tried.

Since there didn't seem to be any end in sight to Sue's bouncing, Gun Smith and Chuck and Moon Hennessey thought they might just as well set out for the I. X. L. ranch. There was nothing they could do and the entire household was so completely disrupted that they were famished for something to eat. Besides, there might be a stampede on back home or something worse. Pecos gave them his permission to go, and as soon as they were out of reach of Pinnacle Mountain they began to laugh themselves sick. Gun Smith started, remarking with straight face:

"Slue-foot Sue is sure one prize *bouncin'* bride!"

Mushmouth burst out with a verse of *The Little Black Bull Came Bawling Down the Mountain.*

Rusty Peters shouted:

> "I'm a riding son of thunder of the sky,
> I'm a broncho twisting wonder on the fly.
> Hey, you earthlings, shut your winders,
> We're a-ripping clouds to flinders—
> If the blue-eyed darling kicks at you, you die."

As he finished, Chuck took it up:

"I want to be a cowboy and with the cowboys stand,
Big spurs upon my bootheels and a lasso in my hand;
My hat broad-brimmed and belted upon my head I'll place,
And wear my chaparajos with elegance and grace."

"But I won't ever try to ride that skyscrapin' Widow Maker, not after what's happened to the fair Sue," roared Gun Smith. "I love my life too well!"

So the cowboys went joyously back to their work. But back on Pinnacle Mountain Pecos was neither joyous nor happy. After three days of ceaseless watching, he was able to estimate the time it would take Sue to come to rest. During the first, there had been an hour and a half between succeeding rebounds; during the second day an hour and a quarter; and during the third day only an hour. At this rate he could plainly understand that she still had two or three more days to go before stopping.

Night and day Pecos Bill stood and watched helplessly. Each night he built a gypsy fire so that Sue might know he had not deserted her.

At last, at the end of the sixth day, Pecos succeeded in lassoing Sue and in carrying her in to her prostrate mother.

"The wretch! The wretch! The wretch!" snapped the mother.

"Colonel Bill's to blame," insisted my lord.

Slue-foot Sue was too exhausted even to cry. She lay with a wan, helpless, pathetic little smile playing silently around her mouth. After a week or two she began listlessly to talk, but in a strange, quiet, mouse-like whisper. The vivacious, romantic Sue that had been was no more.

"Wouldn't it be best, Pecos, if our marriage were never to take place after all?" she said appealingly one afternoon a week later, as Pecos sat faithfully beside her bed. "You see, I won't want ever to ride a broncho again, nor even look at a catfish. I'm entirely cured. I want to go back with Mother to a world where things are at least partly civilized."

The mother, who was listening, called my lord and His Eminence. Together they decided to release Colonel Bill from all future obligations as regards Sue.

It was another new experience for Pecos Bill when he was obliged to take a lasting farewell of Sue. There were ever so many things he wanted to say, but, like the wise man that he was, he kept them all discreetly under the middle of his tongue.

He kissed Sue's hand in silence, took up his Stetson and walked with mixed feelings out where Widow Maker was patiently waiting. He leapt astride and rode, and rode, and rode, without hesitating, across the endless country. He crossed Canada, skirted the valleys of the Platte, of the Missouri, of the Arkansas, and of the Rio Grande. In silence he rode here and there among the mountains, along the rivers, and across the rolling mesa. And everywhere he went he told his troubles to the Coyotes and the other animals, and they all told him theirs. There wasn't a thing any of them could do about anything.

"But if I can't do anything about Sue, there's plenty else I can turn my hand to," mused Pecos as he rode sadly along.

The first day he amused himself by putting horns on all the toads he met. The second day he put the thorns on the mesquite trees and cactuses. The third day he cried so hard

his tears started the Butte Falls in Montana. The fourth day
he used up all the prickly pear leaves in Idaho wiping his eyes,
they smarted so. The fifth day he turned all the corn flowers
and blue bottles into bachelor's buttons.

When Pecos Bill finally rode into the I. X. L. ranch he was
wistful and sad. Something fine had gone from his life, never
to return.

"Oh, no, it isn't as you think," Pecos replied when Gun
Smith asked him why he looked so down and out. "Fate never
intended me to be a husband. I'm awfully glad Slue-foot Sue
and the others found it out so soon. I just wasn't cut out for a
husband, you might say. No, boys, that's not what's got me
downhearted.

"What's really troubling me, Gun Smith, is the coming of
the Nesters and the Hoe-men," Pecos continued. "Everywhere, by the side of the Platte and down the Missouri and
across the Arkansas and along the Rio Grande, civilization is
on the march. Covered wagons and shacks are multiplying
by leaps and bounds, barbed wire is being stretched, and home-
steads are becoming permanent! The days of the free grass
range are gone forever!"

"You don't mean it!" Gun Smith exclaimed, not sure he
could believe his ears.

"The railroads and the barbed wire are turning the trick.
I've just come from visiting all the range land and I know
what I'm talking about. It won't be long now until we'll have
got our herds together and rushed our cattle to the nearest
packing house. Of course, there are a few things we'll have
to do before we start the drive."

Pecos Bill concluded by singing a song he had improvised
along the way:

"Oh, it's squeak! squeak! squeak!
  Hear them stretching of the wire.
The Nester brand is on the land;
  I reckon I'll retire.
'Twas good to live when all the sod
  Without no fence or fuss,
Belonged in partnership to God,
  The Government and us.
While progress toots her brassy horn
  And makes her Hoe-men buzz,
I thank the Lord I wasn't born
  No later than I wuz."

PART IV

THE PASSING OF PECOS BILL

XVII.

RUSTLERS DELUXE

With the passing of time, especially the time Pecos was riding over to Pinnacle Mountain to see Sue, the cattle in his herds increased like guinea pigs. No one had any idea of their number. It got more and more difficult for the outriders to keep the steers from wandering and straying. The Government needed more and more beef for its Army Posts and for the Indian tribes that were herded together on the Reservations. In this situation, politicians began to rustle cattle. And the biggest politician of the lot was Major Duval, the lord of the mountain.

Major Duval bribed all the officers of the law in his section of the country and kept Justice playing at Blind Man's Buff.

In fact, the Major had such a taking way with him that his cattle got to be known everywhere as the Miracle Herd. He had a hidden valley of blue grass, inside a great box canyon among the mountains. This was quite similar to Hell's Gate Gulch, except that it was ten times as large. And the miracle in it was this—no matter how many steers he sold to the Government, his herd never got a bit smaller.

The Major and his confidential henchmen had a little saying of their own that they enjoyed repeating: "Eatin' one's own meat is worse than eatin' poison."

These men not only stole cattle, they also traveled great distances to gather in hogs for their own use. They did love the taste of bacon between their teeth.

One day a Hoe-man or Homesteader—that's what the cow-men called the families who were beginning to take up the land for permanent farms—tracked his own hogs to the Major's ranch. He was expert at trailing and he was sure he had found the thieves. Imagine his surprise at meeting what seemed a neatly dressed gentleman of leisure. The Major greeted the Hoe-man cordially and told him to look around the premises until he had satisfied himself that the hogs were not at the Miracle Ranch. After the man admitted he must be mistaken, the Major invited him to dinner. The Homesteader innocently partook of his own meat and praised his host for the wonderful table he set. After he had gone, Major Duval and his henchmen doubled over with laughter at their clever deception.

"The only reason we didn't kill him," Duval told his scouts who came in later, "was because we want him to live long enough to raise one more litter of pigs for us."

As time went on, Major Duval and his rustlers became more and more daring in their raids upon the cattle of neighboring herds. They knew that they had the Judge and the attorneys on their side and so they feared neither man nor the devil.

Now the Major had for some time been cutting out the choicest of Pecos Bill's steers. Pecos Bill's outriders themselves had known this, but hadn't said a word, for they were afraid Pecos would think they were neglecting their duty. Besides, Pecos Bill's thoughts had been too much concerned with Sue for him to bother about a few stolen steers, more or less.

Suddenly things came to an acute crisis. Major Duval's men accidentally came face to face with three of Pecos Bill's outriders. Shots were exchanged and one of Major Duval's henchmen was left dead on the range.

This happening so enraged Major Duval that he planned immediate revenge. He called together a dozen of his most daring outlaws and the posse rode straight in the direction of Pecos Bill's ranch. They were prepared neither to give nor to take quarter.

These men quickly killed the first two of Pecos Bill's outriders they happened to meet. "Shootin's purty fair this mornin'," they laughed as they rode forward.

"Could be a lot better!" cackled Puke, the leader of the posse.

And then unexpectedly they came upon Pee-wee. He had taken off his shirt and, for the minute, had laid aside his gun and was enjoying a morning bath in a quiet little pool of sparkling water.

"Stick 'em up!" shouted Puke.

Pee-wee turned quickly and, seeing his danger, dove under water, coming up next to where he had left his gun. He wasn't one to allow himself to be captured alive and tortured by any crowd of bullies. As he rose to lay his hand on his faithful weapon he was riddled with a dozen bullets.

"Huntin's gettin' better fast," laughed Puke.

"Yes," grunted Polly, "but let's be roundin' up some of these steers before we meet the enemy in full force."

"It's sense you're talkin' this time," answered Puke. "Let's get goin'."

Soon the posse had cut out a thousand of Pecos Bill's choicest steers and was urging them in the direction of their Miracle Herd.

Puke, the bully, rode in silence for two or three hours. He seemed to be weighing something very deeply in his mind. Finally he turned to the man next him and said:

"Say, Polly."

"Yes, Puke."

"You know what?"

"No, Puke, I don't."

"Then I'll tell you. The Major's Old Rye has it twenty ways over any brand o' squirrel whiskey in the whole range country. A nip or two would taste mighty good just about now. You know what, when I get these snailin' critters turned in with the Miracle Herd, I mean to drink down a full quart at a gulp, raw!"

It was two days later that Chuck found Pee-wee's body. Pee-wee's calico pony seemed not fully to understand. He was nibbling the grass and affectionately nosing the body and was hungry for human company.

It was easy for Chuck to unravel the tragedy. He found
Pee-wee's shirt and gun beside the pool of sparkling water.
He studied the footprints of the strange horses. One was
larger than the others and toed in slightly with its left hind
foot. Yes, these ruffians were from Major Duval's ranch and
were still working to increase the size of the Miracle Herd.

Chuck hurried to the ranch house, notified Pecos Bill and
Gun Smith, and together they rode back, carrying a shovel.

Chuck dug a rude grave, while Pecos Bill and Gun Smith
wrapped Pee-wee's body in his blanket and tenderly lowering
it into the ground, then filled in the grave with earth.

When they had finished they stood a minute awkwardly
wiping their foreheads and dangling their hats and wishing
that someone was present who could rightly speak for them.

After a strained minute, Pecos Bill pronounced the sim-
ple eulogy: "Pee-wee, we leave you to God and the free grass
prairie. Good-bye, Pee-wee."

As they turned to ride quietly away, Gun Smith said with
force: "Pee-wee, in spite of everything, you was a man!"

When Gun Smith and Chuck had finished telling Pecos
everything concerning Major Duval and his Miracle Ranch,
Pecos thought a moment and then said quietly:

"I think I'll just take a run down there tomorrow morning
and see what's going on."

"You take your life in your hands if you go," Gun Smith
cautioned. "They're heartless desperadoes."

"Well, I've always taken it, haven't I, and I've always
brought it back, too, haven't I?" Pecos Bill laughed.

"But this is different," Gun Smith insisted. "Do you understand this is the most venomous nest of reptiles in all the
Southwest range country?"

"I do," Pecos smiled grimly.

"This Major Duval has used brains in buildin' up his business. He's herded together all the worst outlaw adventurers, the most fearless gunmen he can find. He's bought out the porcupine Judges and the civet cat Attorneys, you understand. He's got justice securely inside his noose, I'm tellin' you."

"Give me an extra gun and plenty of bullets and my long rope," Pecos Bill answered with as quiet an unconcern as if he had been talking about going out to lasso a maverick. "I'll just lope off by myself and see what can be done. You and Chuck and three or four of the others had better ride over a few hours later and see what's happening. I may need your help in bringing back our stolen steers."

Pecos Bill's tone was so matter-of-fact that Gun Smith understood there was no further use in urging caution.

The next day Pecos Bill disguised himself to look like a Missouri greenhorn. He thrust his extra gun deeply into the bosom of his shirt and started loping off afoot with his boots tucked under his arm.

Since he had found Widow Maker, Pecos seldom galloped off alone, for he liked the companionship of the horse. This expedition, however, was of a different sort and he felt that he would succeed better if he went alone and on foot.

He took the easy, springy lope the Coyotes had taught him and in no time at all reached the entrance to Miracle Ranch.

Pecos Bill took care to prevent his being seen. He leapt lightly along the precipitous ledges of rock that bounded the wide valley, until he was in plain view of the pasture lands. At the slightest sound he would stop in his tracks, assume the rigid pose of invisibility and wait until he had assured himself there was no danger.

He could not help gazing at the peaceful herd of beautiful steers eating quietly, and never suspecting they were prisoners. The river ran a curving thread of silver as far as his eye could see, and without his quite knowing it Pecos fed his soul on the silent serene beauty.

He continued leaping lightly from rocky shelf to rocky shelf until he was within a stone's throw of Major Duval's fine appearing ranch house. He then climbed quietly down, pulled on his boots and sauntered carelessly into the very midst of the desperadoes, who were squatting around an open fire, eating their dinner.

Major Duval, who wore his clothes like a gentleman of leisure, was seated in the place of honor, and Puke, his foreman, was at his side, relating the facts concerning the *good day's hunt* they had just enjoyed down in the heart of Pecos Bill's country. Puke was omitting none of the details of Peewee's death. As Pecos broke in upon their quiet he began easily:

"Strangers, howdy! I've entirely lost my way about. I wonder if you can set me right and give me a bite to eat so that I may be striking out for home again."

The men were at first startled to see a stranger so suddenly in their midst. They wondered how much he might have heard of Puke's story. Major Duval, however, held his natural pose of a prince and said kindly:

"Whoever you are, you're welcome. Sit down and eat till you bust."

Pecos Bill's plate was heaped with food and he swallowed his food as if he had not tasted meat for a month of Sundays. As he ate, he made himself right at home. He began by asking a question:

"Whose ranch may this be? Where am I, anyway?"

"I'm Major Duval!" came the quick reply that carried its threat of mortal danger for the stranger. "I'm sometimes called, I understand, the Man of the Mountain. This is the home of Miracle Ranch, if you are anxious to know!"

Pecos Bill gazed at Major Duval with pop-eyed innocence, in spite of the circle of piercing glances, and added:

"I'm positive I ain't never heard the name Duval before, and I don't understand what mountain you're talking about at all. I didn't even know there was such a place around here."

The men around the circle laughed heartily. Here was a greenhorn indeed! How could it possibly happen he had never heard of their outfit?

"Whoever you are, stranger," Major Duval said quietly, "never forget this one thing—Miracle Ranch isn't a place! It's the finest herd of cattle in the world!"

"Well, if you want to know," Pecos answered, holding his disguise perfectly, "I'm a homesteader. I've lately come on from Missouri. The trouble is I brought a half a dozen hogs along with me; but they just naturally vamoosed on me and I'm out now trying to round them up. You see, I trailed them a long ways and then I lost the trail and myself in the bargain. I've wandered around over most of the Southwest Territory the past few days, I guess, and that's why I'm here. I just naturally lost my way right into your ranch."

"You are in a bad fix, indeed," Major Duval replied with a flitting smile. "Well, make yourself at home. We were just in the middle of a good story when you interrupted us. You've heard of Pecos Bill, I suppose?" Major Duval added with a quick rising inflection as he eyed the stranger like a hawk, but there was not the least outward change.

"Pecos Bill, did you say?" Pecos asked with a puzzled look as he scratched his head. "Oh, yes, come to think of it, I did hear a wild yarn or two about him back in Missouri. But I didn't take them seriously at all. I kind of thought they was nothing but big lies. Do you mean to tell me there is a real fellow by the same name?"

"You certainly are a stranger in this part of the country. But you haven't missed anything in not knowing that scoundrel!"

"Is Pecos Bill as bad as all that?" Pecos added.

"Is Pecos Bill bad!" added the Major in a nasty tone of voice. "Pecos Bill is, without the shadow of a doubt, the worst critter in the entire Southwest! He's got all the bad blood of the bull Rattlesnake and all the bad manners of the Skunk and all the bad morals of the cunning Coyote! If you start out and find him, you won't be far from your lost hogs!"

"You don't say!" answered Pecos, pretending to be greatly impressed. "But which way shall I go to find him?"

"The quickest way," smiled the Major, dryly, "is to get out of here as fast as your legs will carry you along—the same trail you followed coming in—and then follow your nose straight till you come to Pecos Bill's I. X. L. Ranch."

"Now, you're only trying to make a fool of me," Pecos replied innocently. "Nobody could possibly follow his nose anywhere in this wilderness, let alone a person who is lost to begin with."

"I'll show you the way," Puke shouted boisterously, and as he spoke he picked up his lariat deftly and without warning flung its noose at Pecos Bill's neck.

"Oh, no you don't!" Pecos shouted as he jumped aside so quickly that the noose fell to the ground. "I'm not Pee-wee."

As Pecos Bill leapt aside, he drew his guns and shot off Puke's trigger fingers. Immediately the air was hopping full of flying lead, and Pecos Bill was forced to dodge so fast that human eyes couldn't follow him. He leapt about so quickly that the men shot on all sides of him, without ever quite hitting him.

And all the while he was dodging, Pecos kept up a barrage of flying bullets from his own guns. He shot off trigger finger after trigger finger from Major Duval and his men. And as the fingers fell the guns fell with them. Whenever Pecos Bill saw a gun pointed directly at him, he promptly spiked it by shooting one of his own bullets down its muzzle. This was one of the little tricks Gun Smith had taught Pecos.

It wasn't long before Major Duval's men were too busy stopping the blood from their missing fingers to pay any too much attention to Pecos Bill. When anyone tried to run, Pecos stopped him in his tracks with the blood call of the Wouser.

As soon as Pecos Bill was out of the middle of his bad fix, he commanded every man to stick 'em up. Then he forced them to march past him while he stripped them of their bowie knives and guns. Soon he had every weapon in a heap beside him.

He next ordered all the men to stand close together. Then he picked up Puke's lariat, enlarged the noose and sent it singing around the middle of the entire posse. This he drew up so tight that the men felt like the broken straws in a bundle of wheat. They were so jammed together they howled in pain. Pecos lashed the end of the lariat securely to a tree.

As soon as he had his job finished he gave a blood-curdling "Ee-Yow!" and in a few minutes Gun Smith and Chuck and a dozen outriders came loping up on their bronchos.

Pecos told them to tie all the guns and bowie knives into bundles. These they lashed to the tail of the saddles. Pecos next told the men to cut out ten thousand steers from the herd.

While this was being done Pecos Bill gave Major Duval and his men a word of advice: "All you've lost of your own is a few trigger fingers. You deserve a lot worse punishment than that. And if ever you set foot on my ranch again, I'll see to it personally you get what is rightly coming to you."

As they were driving their cattle out of the mouth of the canyon, Gun Smith and Chuck met the Judge and the Attorneys, who were riding in for supper. The Judge was accusing the cowboys of being thieves when Pecos Bill arrived.

In two seconds he had his lariat about them, one at a time, and had dragged them to the ground. When they tried to use their guns, Pecos promptly shot off their trigger fingers and took their weapons away from them.

As soon as Pecos Bill had them under control, he sent Gun Smith and Chuck on with the herd, while he took the Judge and the Attorneys back to Major Duval's ranch house. When they saw the Major and his posse roped to a tree like so many outlaw bronchos, they swore vengeance—the vengeance of the law!

Pecos laughed loudly at their mention of the law. He set the Judge on a bench, forced Duval and Puke to plead guilty to a hundred different counts. Then Pecos forced the Judge to hand in a decision of guilty against the entire outfit at Miracle Ranch, himself included. It began, "Know all men by these presents, Whereas...."

When the Judge had finished sentencing each man to banishment from the cattle country for the remainder of his natural life, Pecos added his own conditions:

Pecos Bill roped the Major and his posse to a tree

"If ever Major Duval or Puke or any other of his outfit is caught on Pecos Bill's ranch, or if ever Pecos Bill hears of any of these men robbing any of his neighbors or anybody else, he'll see that they are given such punishment as they will never forget."

After the Judge had finished adding this sentence to what he had already written, Pecos Bill took up the document, lassoed the Judge and the Attorneys around the middle, too, and tied them to another tree. When he had given them a lecture on common decency and honorable Coyote morals, he left them all to get out of their own bad fix the best way they could; then he loped off to join Gun Smith and Chuck.

When he caught up with the herd, Gun Smith and Chuck asked him how he had come out. He answered simply, "I don't think Major Duval, the Man of the Mountain, and his outfit will bother us again . . . at least, not so as you will notice it."

"Why didn't you shoot 'em down like the bad-blooded bull Rattlesnakes they are?" Gun Smith asked.

"I've never yet found it necessary to kill a *human*," answered Pecos Bill dreamily. "That sort of thing may be all right, I suppose, for you fellows who have to kill to save your own life. But so far I've never been reduced to that. I prefer to spike their guns and shoot off their trigger fingers. Among the Coyotes, you know, to have one's toes bitten off by an enemy is the most shocking of any disgrace."

XVIII.

THE GOING OF PECOS AND WIDOW MAKER

Soon Pecos Bill and his men began to talk seriously of the situation Pecos had seen coming on for a long time. The Nesters and Homesteaders were taking up the land on all sides. Civilization was closing in faster and faster. The settlers were stretching barbed wire and announcing, "Private land! No trespassing!" Pecos began to feel crowded and restless, just as his mother had years before when she made her family come along to the Rio Grande. The whole trouble was there wasn't any more open country for Pecos to occupy.

After a long discussion, it was finally decided to cut out from their various herds all the steers that were fit to market and to start them along the trail for Kansas.

After they'd done this, the herd that they got together was so large they didn't even try to make a count of the steers. The best guess they could make was in the neighborhood of thirty-nine million.

"If ever we get these critters to market," Gun Smith declared, "there won't be enough money in the U. S. Treasury to pay for half of them."

"Get them to market!" laughed Pecos Bill. "Why, that's easier than falling off a broncho. Even if we have to cut every barbed wire fence this side of Kingdom Come, we'll see this thing through to the last steer."

The men who were driving arranged themselves around the herd in the shape of a great horseshoe. The cattle thought they were finding their own way, for the end of the horseshoe at the front of the march was, of course, open. Actually the cattle were guarded every step of the way. At the front on either side rode the point or lead men, as they were called. These were followed at regular intervals by the swing or flank riders. These, in turn, were followed by the tail riders, who completed the circle in the rear and kept the straggling drags in the line of march.

Next behind this horseshoe of drivers came Old Satan, the horse wrangler, with his reserve hackamores. And finally, behind these, came Bean Hole with his canvas-covered chuck wagon, drawn by three teams of powerful mules. Pecos Bill knew just how to manage.

As far as the eye could see lumbered the bawling steers.

The scene was like an enormous herd of buffalo of the early days, without beginning or end. The cloud of dust that rose to the heavens shut out the sun. The men felt its stifling oppression as they felt the weltering heat; but they stuck to their several tasks without a word.

First they were parched by the rays of the sun, then they were frozen fording rivers in the gray morning dawn. It was all in the day's work and they were there to see the drive through to Kansas or bust, even though it proved the last piece of work they *ever did*.

When evening came, the chuck wagon was drawn up beside some natural spring of clear running water. Bean Hole would tumble off his high perch and pull down the cover of the great box at the rear of the wagon. This was his pantry.

While the other men rustled wood and lighted the gypsy fire, Bean Hole rattled his kettles. In less time than it takes to tell it, his famous frying-pan bread was piping hot. Bean Hole would yell loud enough to waken the dead:

"Come and take it, or I'll throw it into the fire!"

The men came on the gallop, threw the reins over their ponies' heads, and sat teetering on their haunches in a circle.

After they had eaten the men removed the fifty-pound cow-saddles from their ponies, hobbled them or picketed them out as they preferred. Then they took their fat gray rolls of blankets from the front of Bean Hole's chuck wagon and made their beds under the open sky.

During the evening Rusty Peters would lift many a hoof between his knees and replace a lost shoe. Mushmouth would start his lip-piano with *Rocked in the Cradle of the Deep* or *The Little Roan Bull Came Bawling Down the Mountain,* and Bullfrog Doyle would dance like a drunken hornpiper. Fat

Adams would practice new ways to amuse the men with his shadow boxing. Pretty Pete Rogers would brush the dust and horsehair from his Stetson and swear he was going to turn a tailor's model. Old Satan would recount the good old days when he and his Hellions shot up Dallas.

After the stars were laughing overhead the men would roll themselves in their blankets, lay their heads on their saddles and sleep the sleep of the just. As the softened shadows of the moon fell upon their camp it saw an irregular series of small gray mounds.

Pecos Bill had decided to make the men believe that they themselves were conducting this drive. So he did not do too much; but he was here, there and everywhere. When a stampede threatened, he kept Widow Maker flying around and around the herd, singing soothing songs as he went. The cattle knew what he said and were patient even in a menacing thunder storm.

When a swollen stream was to be crossed, Pecos was there with Widow Maker and his quirt and his rope. He was able to talk to the steers in their own language. The stubborn ones he conquered and the lead cattle he directed to a natural landing place.

When the herd did explode unexpectedly in a wild stampede, Widow Maker and Pecos circled the flying leaders like strokes of greased lightning and soon had the cattle milling round and round in a compact mass.

It was Pecos who in the end saved every impossible situation from becoming a disaster. Without him, Gun Smith and the others would have been powerless to drive such a mighty herd across the open country.

During the first week Gun Smith and his men pushed the

herd to the limit. They were attempting to wear the steers down until they became docile and too tired to attempt a stampede.

Each night, after they had allowed the cattle to graze and drink their fill, the men bedded them down. But this was only the beginning of the night. The men took their turns at watching, riding slowly round and round the herd and singing songs to assure the cattle that there was no danger.

Every morning at sunup the caravan started again. Hour after hour it crawled along at a snail's pace. Late in the afternoon the cattle were driven to rich pastures and allowed to fill up for the early part of the night. The men considered themselves fortunate if they found they had made ten or a dozen miles in as many hours.

The monotony was broken by the changing country and by the weather. Nearly every day there was at least one river to ford and at frequent intervals there were thunderstorms of varying intensity.

The men could never quite predict just what the steers would do in a new situation. Sometimes they chose to be stubborn and sometimes they decided, in spite of everything, to go in the wrong direction. And occasionally the herd actually exploded like a piece of shrapnel. It was then that the nerve of every man was a-tingle. At times, in desperation, the crazed, frothing leaders of the stampede had to be shot. Always the task was a real cowman's job.

It was the business of the men to sense and anticipate every move of the cattle and to catch every electric spark of feeling that passed through the herd before it had done any damage. Otherwise, it was impossible to cope with the sudden changes in the temper of the steers. The cowboy had little time for sleep during the drive. He always had to be on the alert and had ever to prove himself the master of whatever situation might arise.

As the drive progressed it became necessary to send at least three or four outriders ahead to prepare the way. There were Nester shacks to be avoided and wire fences to be cut.

Scarcely a day passed that some Nester's cattle did not come bawling into the herd. Closely following the cattle usually came the Nester himself, demanding that his cattle be immediately cut out from among the steers.

"But we're runnin' short-handed," Gun Smith would explain.

"You're trespassing and I'll have the law on you," the Nester would threaten hotly.

"Besides, the steers are tired and are gettin' thin from the daily drive. We can't afford to begin ginnin' them around merely to cut out your few cattle," Gun Smith would explain quietly.

The Nester would become more and more angry and unreasonable, until Pecos Bill would come forward and pay the Nester two or three times what his cattle were worth. Sometimes the Nester would keep on being so nasty and threatening that Pecos Bill would be forced to drive him away with harsh words. He never, however, failed to leave money to pay for whatever damage he had done.

The great herd naturally acted as a mighty magnet. The cattle of the Nesters and Hoe-men were but particles of iron filings in its presence. The cattle would come running and bawling and in a few minutes become so scattered among the steers that they never again could be found.

As the days went on the herd thus gradually became larger

instead of smaller. With Pecos always on hand to round up
the strays and to put fresh energy into the drags, there was
little chance of losing as many cattle as the number that was
added.

One evening after the herd was safely bedded down, the
men gathered for two or three hours around the fire beside
the chuck wagon and gave their time over to tall talk. Many
were the wild adventures they retold. After a time, as the
moon arose and cast its weird shadows, Pecos Bill told his
men what he had on his mind:

"My merry men, my Texas cowpunching is through. When
we've got the herd through to Kansas City, we'll all split the
profits. If you boys'll use your heads and go back and buy
up the homesteaded lands, you'll be able to combine them
into sizeable ranches. You can fence yourselves in with barbed
wire and be free from the swarming Nesters and Hoe-men.
There's plenty of cattle playing around back at our old ranch
to furnish you all the foundation stock you'll ever need."

"But what are ye goin' to do?" Gun Smith asked curiously.

"That's not quite decided," Pecos answered simply. "You
see, it's like this. Widow Maker and me have got to have room
to kick up our heels, and there's not room for us any longer
in Texas!"

"But you've got to stick with the outfit!" Gun Smith urged.

"Boys, I'm sure sorry to leave you," Pecos answered with
intense feeling. "You've been real friends to me and there's
no wealth in this world quite equal to one's friends. When I
came among you I was suspicious of all *humans*. Among the
wild animals, *humans* have a black reputation, as you well
know. I have lived long enough with you to know that human
nature, at its best, is the very best there is anywhere. And so

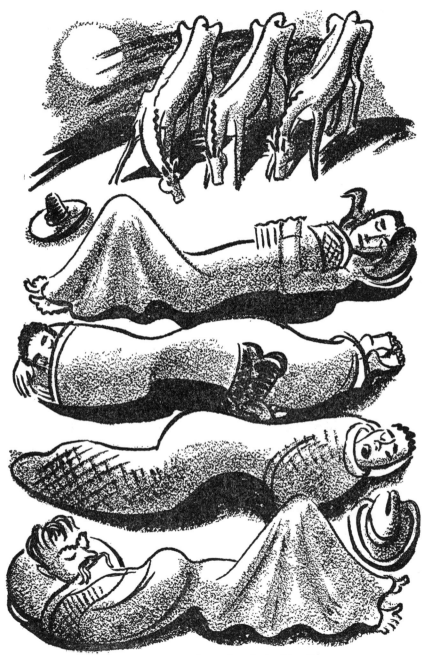

The men rolled up in their blankets

I'm glad I left the Coyotes and came to live with you."

"We're all sure glad that Chuck found you," Gun Smith declared.

"The Coyotes, among themselves, are a fine race," Pecos continued, "and so are the Bears among themselves. The same is true of the Mountain Lions and the Bob Cats and even of the Wousers. Experience's taught me that no race at its best is quite so good as the best *humans* of the ranches. At its worst, no race—I make no exception even of the bad-blooded, poisonous Reptiles—is worse than what in the Coyote language is called the *inhumans!*"

"How do you hope to better yourself any by leavin' us?" Gun Smith asked. "And if you don't better yourself, you're sure not goin' to better the rest of us any."

"As I have said before, there's not room enough in Texas for Widow Maker and me. We are both freeborn and we just naturally can't stay fenced in."

When the men tired of their talk, they rolled up in their blankets and slept through the night. Next morning they had all forgotten what Pecos had said. He'd never leave them, they were sure of that. All but Gun Smith, that is, and Gun Smith wondered.

After three and a half months of faithful driving, the great unwieldy herd was at last brought to the gates of Kansas City. As usual Pecos Bill was making geography. The path that the herd had just made through the wild country later came to be known as the Chisholm Trail.

As used as the natives had become to seeing many cattle, they now had to admit they had never before seen a real herd of steers. "Three cheers for Pecos Bill!" every man, woman and child in Kansas City shouted as the herd came thundering by.

The gates of the slaughterhouse were swung wide, and the pens were soon full to overflowing; and still the herd outside the pens extended for miles in every direction.

The managers of the packing houses were forced to enlarge their factories three different times, and to put on two extra shifts of men. They also started a gang of fifty men building extra pens; but in spite of everything they could do, Pecos Bill and his men were obliged to drive the greater part of the herd out on the plains again. The remaining steers were pastured over almost all the Missouri Valley.

By the time they were returned they had eaten practically every blade of grass so close that even a sheep wouldn't have been tempted by what was left. For years the region was set down in the geography as the Great American Desert, and it is often rumored to this day that this is the reason why the soil in certain parts of this valley is still so thin and poor.

The final result of the slaughter of all these countless steers was that the price of beef throughout the United States, Canada, Great Britain, Germany, France, Italy, and even China and the South Sea Islands, broke sharply and fell as much as ten cents on the pound, due to the enormous oversupply. It is the common belief in certain sections of the country, that some of these same cans of tinned beef can still be found on the shelves of merchants in out of the way places. And it was through the sale of this same meat that one of our national packing companies first became an international institution.

When the last steer was finally turned into the pens and the money divided, each man found himself wealthy.

"Do as I've told you," said Pecos, "and you'll never be sorry. You cowmen keep all your money and I'll spend whatever's necessary to entertain these stiff-collar city dudes."

The men followed Pecos Bill's advice, and that is the very reason there are so many Dude ranches even now scattered across the western part of Texas, and north as far as Montana.

After they had finished the business transaction, Pecos Bill and his men were in a holiday mood. They decided to give Kansas City the first real Wild West Show that had ever been invented, outside the heart of the Southwest.

Gun Smith and Old Satan and their cowmen did all sorts of fancy riding and fancy roping. They *bulldogged* and *hog-tied* steers. Pecos mounted Widow Maker and Gun Smith rode beside him, and these two did shooting from horseback such as was never seen anywhere on this planet before or since.

Old Satan and his Cavalrymen showed everybody exactly how to shoot up a frontier town with desperado daring. And when Old Satan got off his speech about Hell's Gate Gulch, the audience was sure he actually was as tough as he sounded.

Mushmouth did the act of his life by playing *The Little Roan Bull* on one lip-piano in one corner of his mouth, and *O Bury Me Not on the Lone Prairie* on the other. And at the same time he sang the words of *Rocked in the Cradle of the Deep* with the middle of his tongue.

Bullfrog Doyle, not to be outdone, danced one of Mushmouth's tunes with one leg, and the other two with the other leg. Everybody wondered how his body could stand up under the terrific strain. They thought that one or the other of his legs would surely fly off into space any second.

Rusty Peters carried on a shadow boxing match with Fat Adams. Fat would dodge Rusty's sledgehammer blows, turn sidewise so that the audience could not see him. Rusty would then brag that he had knocked Fat into the middle of the next new moon. When the audience was beginning to be-

lieve this, Fat would step around behind Rusty, turn so that
he could again be seen, and laugh to split his sides.

When the show was over, the natives were satisfied that
this was the most wonderful outfit of cowmen ever assembled.

Before he left town for good, Pecos Bill decided to give
Kansas City the surprise of its young life. He felt hurt to hear
the men in dudish city clothes make so many belittling remarks about cowpunchers.

"I'll teach some of these smarties to respect an honest cowman before the evening's over," he told his men. "You just
keep quiet and watch what happens."

Soon after nightfall Pecos started down the street to see the
sights. As he passed a crowd that loitered in front of the first
saloon he reached, a smart Aleck made a nasty remark about
the passing long-horn maverick. Pecos turned on his heel
and faced the speaker squarely: "No offense intended, I hope,"
he smiled.

"Who do you think you are to be talking to me, you young
fleabitten maverick! Get back to the ranch where you belong,
and tell your troubles to the yowling Coyotes!"

Pecos took a threatening step in the speaker's direction, and
the bully flashed his gun. Then before anybody quite came
to his senses, Pecos had spiked the offender's gun, had shot
off his trigger finger, had galloped around the corner and was
completely out of sight.

By loping at full speed down a back alley Pecos reached
another part of the street far ahead of the news of his recent
fracas. The next minute, as he sauntered harmlessly along,
looking at nothing in particular, another smart Aleck and
bully insulted him.

Pecos as usual took his instant revenge, then vanished to

still a different part of the town. Within less than an hour Pecos had the entire city agog. As the shooting frays came in rapid succession to the ears of the police they gave instant chase, for they could not allow all their local bullies to go down in such defeat before a mere cowpuncher.

With no knowledge of what was happening, Pecos Bill appeared as if by magic in widely separated places. His movements were so incredibly rapid that the Police Department was always at least three jumps behind in the race.

Toward the end of the evening Pecos came face to face with Knockdown Buckner, the most famous two-fisted giant of the entire range country. Knockdown had the bad habit of swatting every bully he met with his sledgehammer blows. When he ran out of material around the saloons he leapt astride his broncho and rode out for adventure. He kept in training by knocking down every Indian warrior of every tribe he happened to meet. Usually he knocked down the Chieftain of the tribe three times, just for good measure.

Pecos knew Knockdown Buckner at first glance, for he was the only man in the Southwest who did not carry on his person at least one Colt revolver.

After exchanging gruff greetings, Pecos said coolly: "Well, Buckner, come on. I'll give you the first three swats!"

"Three, did you say!" Knockdown shouted in anger. "You puny cayuse, why, I can knock you down with a quarter of one punch."

"I wouldn't brag about it just yet," Pecos smiled.

This so completely enraged Knockdown that he gave a terrific lunge and shot his fist out like a thunderbolt. Pecos used the foot work that Grandy had taught him when he was a boy, and leapt completely out of Knockdown's reach.

The result of the terrific blow into empty space was that Knockdown threw his good right arm out of the socket at the shoulder, lost his balance completely, and fell heavily on his face. He staggered to his feet, and in his rage again went for Pecos. This time he threw his good left arm out of joint at the elbow, and again battered his nose on the sidewalk.

"You're about the craziest cayuse I ever met," Pecos taunted. "Why, you couldn't hit the side of a maverick corral if you was inside and had the gate barred. You aren't worth a good swat, but here's a little love pat for remembrance."

Then Pecos hit the dazed Knockdown square in the middle of his nose. This blackened both his eyes and considerably altered his face. "Now you'll know how it feels to be knocked down."

The next minute Pecos had again disappeared.

The Police Department, in despair, finally called out the City Fire Department to help them. A general search was started and the only reason it was not more successful was because there were so very many saloons and bullies.

Before midnight Pecos had visited every street where idle men loitered before saloons, and as a result, all the surgeons in town were kept busy for the next fortnight mending hands that had lost trigger fingers. Never before nor since was there such a sickly lot of bullies in the world at any one time.

In utter despair the Chief of Police issued the order to arrest every cowpuncher at sight. It was thus that Gun Smith, Old Satan and all their men were innocently caught in the dragnet and forced to spend the night in jail. What these innocents said about Police Departments has become classic. Scarcely a day passes but that somewhere, some unlucky harmless person is locked up in the place of the real lawbreaker, and always these innocent people repeat the same language that Gun Smith and Old Satan this night invented. It is lucky for the officers of the law that this has never been set down in print.

Before they arrested Moon Hennessey, he had consumed all the hard liquor in three different saloons and had actually drunk his weight in squirrel whiskey. While Gun Smith and Old Satan and the rest were fuming and sweating, and speaking all manner of evil about their oppressors, Pecos Bill was finishing with the last remaining bully. He now waved his hat in triumph, and loped off to find Widow Maker. As he ran he laughed:

"I've started something they won't soon forget in these parts. They'll look the next cowpuncher over twice before they attack him!"

With the entire city out to catch Pecos Bill, and with nearly every private citizen sworn in as an officer, he rode serenely off into the night.

A reward of five thousand dollars was offered for his arrest, and many different detective agencies wasted years in vain pursuit of him, but he was never caught.

XIX.

THE FABLED DEMIGOD

When no one was able to capture Pecos Bill and claim the reward, there came with time a growing discussion among his cowmen as to what had happened to their remarkable friend.

Gun Smith and Moon Hennessey argued day after day, month after month, year after year, without reaching an agreement.

Moon maintained that when he went back to them, the approved packs of Coyotes called Pecos Bill to account for helping to bring about the rapid increase in cowmen and Nesters and Hoe-men.

"It ain't accordin' to reason they'd let Pecos Bill off easy," Moon Hennessey argued. "He did help bring the railroads, and the barbed wire. These all come about through his teachin' the cowmen improved methods of rearin' their stock, and runnin' their business. If it hadn't been for Pecos and all his inventions the wild varmints would have had much better huntin', wouldn't they? And wouldn't that make the varmints angry?"

"What do you think the Coyotes did to Pecos then?" Gun Smith asked.

"Well, no doubt, they did a-plenty. Like as not they pounced on him and Widow Maker and made a hearty meal of their carcasses."

"Don't you fool yourself into believin' any such nonsense," Gun Smith countered. "Pecos wasn't the kind o' greenhorn to let any bunch of Coyotes stop his stampedin' to safety. Mounted on the hurricane deck of Widow Maker, he'd never stand for any pack of brute varmints capturin' him, no difference how wild and woolly they were."

"Well, then, what do you think did happen to him?" Moon Hennessey urged.

"I think there was a big argument all right," Gun Smith explained. "But just about the time the varmints was ready to close in on him, Pecos give the word to Widow Maker and away they loped, thunderin' like mad for freedom. The Coyotes would, of course, give chase; but after a day or two, by the time they'd completely lost the trail, Pecos would have been five or six thousand miles away, laughing a provokin' kind of laugh to find how conceited Coyotes and Wolves are anyhow, to think they could ever catch the likes of him and Widow Maker."

"And what then?" Moon urged him to continue.

"Well, Pecos Bill most likely found some vast hidden, sodded, box canyon among the impassable mountains, with an entrance as crooked as the devil's walkin' stick, that no one else will ever discover. By this time he's got it stocked with the biggest herd of longhorn cattle in the entire world. Yes, and I'll bet my bottom dollar he wasn't away a month before he'd gone back to fetch Slue-foot Sue to dwell in his paradise. What with lassooin' His Eminence to perform the ceremony and ridin' off with his bride, he was too busy to tell us of his intentions. Sue was some woman, mind you, and long before Pecos Bill went back for her she'd got over the slight scare Widow Maker give her when he bucked her into the sky. Pecos Bill has gentled her the finest calico broncho you can imagine, and together they're hittin' it off in a regular cowpuncher's paradise."

"If all this was true," Moon argued, "wouldn't he come back to fetch us to be a part of his outfit? Pecos Bill wasn't the kind of fellow to be alone, and you know it!"

"Yes, but you know Slue-foot Sue, too. She'd have her say about that. Why, they wouldn't have any use for our outfit. The box canyon would be surrounded with mountains on all sides and there would be springs of sparklin' water. What would two people as happy as Pecos and Sue want with a bunch of roughnecks like us around? They've got a regular paradise—an improved sort of Garden of Eden. Varmints like us, Moon, would be worse'n bad-blooded snakes. We wouldn't fit in with that scenery, I'll say we wouldn't. Besides, Pecos and Sue are, like as not, raisin' a regular outfit for themselves.

They've got ten or a dozen boys of their own by this time, or I'm a busted broncho."

"You sure have got some imagination," Moon Hennessey commented. "And I say you're dead wrong. Pecos Bill's and Widow Maker's bones are bleachin' in the sun somewheres, and we could find 'em if we only knew where to look."

So the argument ran. The only proof anybody had was his own individual opinion. The longer the men argued the firmer each was in his own mind that he was right.

This much is certain. Wherever cowmen are gathered, and whenever cowpunchers meet, to this day Pecos Bill is among them. He has become the demigod of the ranch. When the herd suddenly explodes and starts a wild stampede, the cowpuncher whispers to himself as he puts spur to his faithful broncho, "If Pecos Bill was only here with his lasso to rope the whole infernal herd with a single toss of his noose, wouldn't he bring the old reprobates back together in a hurry!"

When the best of the outlaw bronchos is *skyscraping* and *sunfishing* and *cake walking*, whoever happens to be on the hurricane deck is sure to shout to himself: "Buck your fill, you lazy varmint! If I was only aboard Widow Maker it would be some sensation to be bucked over the top of Pike's Peak or into the face of the Moon!"

And when the men are doing their best fancy roping, someone is sure to remark: "Well, that isn't so bad for a greenhorn. But remember this, it isn't touchin' a candle to what Pecos Bill used to do left-handed with his eyes shut!"

Whether it be at Cheyenne, or Fort Worth, or Denver, or Winnipeg, or Grangeville, or Kearney, or Salinas, or Ukiah, or Walla Walla, it is always the same. Wherever is celebrated *Frontier Days* or the *Cattleman's Carnival* or the *Festival of*

the Mountain and Plain or the *Stampede* or the *Border Days*
or the *Frontier Roundup* or the *Rodeo* or the *Cowboys' Convention,* Pecos Bill is there busting the bronchos and bulldogging the steers and wielding the magic rope. In every man's
imagination this marvelous cowman rides unmolested to glory
and to undying fame.